★ ★ ★

# Our Healing Farm

### Presents a Holy Spirit-Led Study

# Say Howdy to Healing and Hope!

## A GUIDE TO RESTORATION THROUGH FAITH AND HORSES

FBEAP CERTIFIED
✝
OUR HEALING FARM
HOLY SPIRIT-LED
CARO, MI
OURHEALINGFARM.COM

## WRITTEN BY MELISSA PRUSINSKI
### Faith-Based Equine Assisted Philosophy
### Founded by Elaine Davis of Unbridled™

# Dedication

I dedicate this book to Blake, Linden, and Sutton. Your support throughout my healing journey has meant the world to me, and I truly appreciate how you've inspired me to strive for a better version of myself. I could not have written this book without your unwavering encouragement and understanding during this process. Thank you for being there for me every step of the way. I love you so much!

Also, I offer up a special thanks to Elaine Davis and Door of Hope Ministries.

I will be forever thankful for the dedicated research and the countless hours invested into FBEAP, Unbridled™. I am also grateful for the Christian approach to healing from trauma that is available through Door of Hope Ministries. Because of both organizations' efforts, I have gained invaluable knowledge about healing that has truly changed my life. I hope this learning can positively impact countless others who come to Our Healing Farm *and* those who use this study guide in their own hometowns!

With love,

# Disclaimer

The content provided in this book and any experiences or activities conducted at Our Healing Farm LLC—including those involving horses—are intended for informational purposes only.

We are not medical professionals. Melissa Prusinski is a certified FBEAP facilitator who collaborates with the unseen facilitator, the Holy Spirit. Nothing in this book or shared during any farm visit or activity should be viewed as medical guidance, diagnosis, or treatment. Always seek advice from a qualified healthcare provider before making any health-related decisions.

This book shares the author's opinions and insights, which are intended to be helpful and supportive. However, please note that at Our Healing Farm LLC, we are not licensed therapists or mental health professionals. Nothing in this book or study guide or any farm-related experience should be considered a substitute for professional counseling, therapy, or medical treatment.

While we strive for accuracy and clarity, we make no guarantees or warranties—expressed or implied—regarding the completeness, reliability, or accuracy of the information contained herein. We are not responsible for any errors, omissions, or consequences that may arise from using this material.

Misuse of any of the book's content is solely the user's responsibility. We are not liable for any outcomes, damages, or injuries resulting from improper or unintended material application.

By reading this book or participating in any activities at Our Healing Farm LLC—including interaction with or use of horses—you acknowledge and accept that you do so voluntarily and at your own risk. Horses are large, potentially unpredictable animals, and while we take reasonable safety precautions, we are not liable for any injury, loss, or damages of any kind.

Engagement with any of our materials or activities constitutes acceptance of this disclaimer and a full release of liability for the author, Melissa Prusinski; farm owners; employees; and affiliates.

# Table of Contents

# Introduction

Howdy, friend! I'm incredibly proud of you for taking this important step to join Our Healing Farm's herd. You may be joining our herd in person at our farm out in Michigan or using this book to guide yourself through healing and restoration right in your own hometown. Either way, I know that God the Father, the Son, and the Holy Spirit will be with you as you seek them. May you embark on a transformative journey led by the Holy Spirit as your partner!

## Healing and Hope

Our Healing Farm started as an online platform to share my healing journey from chronic Lyme disease. Early on, I was focused on healing my body, but during sleepless nights filled with cries for relief, I realized the need to address my spirit and soul as well.

The Holy Spirit guided me to explore using horses in a healing ministry, which led me to Elaine Davis of Unbridled™. I didn't know it at the beginning, but taking that step of faith brought me the healing and hope I needed most.

Through Elaine Davis's teachings, my connection to Door of Hope Ministries, and insights from studying various books (particularly the works of James Wilder and Karl Lehman), my mind and soul have begun to heal profoundly. I also want to tip my hat to Life Model Works™ because Our Healing Farm has been based on The Life Model presented by their organization. God has revealed that living a life led by the Holy Spirit is essential to achieving true joy and happiness. I have come to understand the significance of integrating faith with the science of our bodies for whole body healing.

If you have a pulse, you have healing to accomplish. We all face challenging times in life, and none of us are untouched by pain. If you're one of the fortunate few who feel you need less healing, I'm truly glad you're here. It's important to embrace this way of living, as we all deserve joy in our lives. Those who are struggling around us can greatly benefit from a compassionate mentor to support them through their healing journey. That's why this study is meant for everyone!

I'm incredibly proud of you for taking this important step to join Our Healing Farm's herd. May you embark on a transformative journey led by the Holy Spirit!

Are you ready to take a healing trail ride? Giddy up!

# What Is FBEAP?

You may already have an understanding or knowledge surrounding Faith-Based Equine Assisted Philosophy. If not, this part of the Introduction will be especially helpful.

Elaine Davis, the founder of Unbridled™, began this organization back in 2005 and has led certification seminars since 2007.

Our Healing Farm was certified to facilitate Faith-Based Equine Assisted Philosophy programs in 2022. We understand the deep challenges that many face, and we are proud to be certified in Faith-Based Equine Assisted Philosophy (FBEAP). This approach has had a transformative impact on my life, and I want to share that hope with others. When I embarked on my journey to become certified in FBEAP Trauma Recovery, I was surprised to discover my own need for healing. As a Christian, I struggled for nearly two decades to break free from patterns of behavior that weighed heavily on my heart. It became clear to me that I was carrying unresolved wounds that needed to be addressed.

Trauma is a very real experience, and if ignored, it can leave lasting wounds. During my certification, I discovered a new way of understanding healing. I learned that God created horses to embody traits that reflect Jesus and encourage us to look forward, strive for growth, and push through the weight of our past that may feel overwhelming. When clients come to the farm, we combine the teachings from this study of our Christian beliefs and doctrine along with the meaningful FBEAP exercises. Together, we work toward breakthroughs that can truly change lives.

FBEAP is the only Christ-centered equine assisted learning training program available, and it is designed to support individuals like you in identifying the lies you may have unintentionally accepted from the Enemy. Together, we can replace those lies with the healing truths that set us free. Our program encourages you to discern and respond to the gentle guidance of the Holy Spirit, fostering a path toward healing and renewal.

FBEAP is founded upon the Word of God. It applies EAL/EAP (equine assisted learning/ equine assisted physiotherapy) on top of the Word of God and is directed by the Holy Spirit. It addresses the whole person: body, soul, and spirit. We are a triune being, created in the image of God. In order to experience the freedom that Jesus died for us to know, we must address the whole person.[1] FBEAP is based on six different philosophies that are explained in the foundational work by Elaine Davis:

---

1      Elaine Davis, *Foundations* (Unbridled™, 2012), 15.

- **Pressure/Pain**
- **Confrontation**
- **Relationship Zones**

- **The Re-Circle**
- **Push/Pull**
- **Attention and At Ease**[2]

In this book, we will journey together through these six FBEAP principles in more detail.

You may be wondering, "Do I need to have horses to benefit from this study?" I want to assure you that you absolutely do not! While the most enriching experience would be to visit the farm and to participate in a group setting with the FBEAP horse exercises, I understand that not everyone has access to that opportunity. You can still experience profound healing and a meaningful connection to horses through the insights in this book, even without a nearby FBEAP facilitator.

It is my heartfelt hope that this book will inspire many to seek certification with Unbridled™ so that we can spread the benefits of FBEAP further and wider. The intention behind releasing this book on a larger scale is to help more people find healing—because I truly believe that everyone deserves this journey. God wants His people to heal!

## Why a Horse?

Horses are honest creatures. They have the ability to sense our feelings, and when that is combined with the power of the Holy Spirit, it can lead us to remarkable "ah-ha" experiences.

Horses have exceptional vision. With 360-degree awareness and strong peripheral sight, horses are able to detect important cues. Horses exist entirely in the present, are consistently honest, and are always eager to advance. They do not dwell on the past or wish for different outcomes. As Davis and Anderson have explained, horses react positively to genuine actions, and they progress forward.[3]

As an FBEAP facilitator, I am fully aware of the knowledge gained through the work of Unbridled™. This work has also shown how invaluable horses can be for the many layers of healing that are possible for men and women.

---

2      Davis, *Foundations,* 22–23.
3      Elaine Davis and Ruth Anderson, *Gal-Up Hope Trail* (Unbridled™, 2022), 8–9.

## What Are We Not?

FBEAP facilitators are not therapists. As facilitators, we use exercises with the horse that allow the Holy Spirit to address the client in His timing. We let God do the work and only speak when we feel led. We do not believe in re-traumatizing a person. When we facilitate sessions with clients on Our Healing Farm, we don't believe in getting to the bottom of everything right away; healing often comes in layers. As Christians, we can rely on the Holy Spirit revealing truths in His time, not ours. FBEAP facilitators will not ask intrusive questions to try to dig deep with the client. We know that those kinds of questions can traumatize them more if they are not healed enough to deal with the questions or answers that come with them.

## The Word and the Herd

As it says in *Gal-Up Hope Trail*, "If we see it in the Word and see it in the herd, we know this principle will give us life."[4] Interestingly, Jesus and His apostles moved in Scripture much like horses do—always moving forward. Paul said this so perfectly in his letter to the Philippians when he wrote, "No, dear brothers and sisters, I have not achieved it, but I focus on this one thing: Forgetting the past and looking forward to what lies ahead, I press on to reach the end of the race and receive the heavenly prize for which God, through Christ Jesus, is calling us" (Philippians 3:13–14). This study aims to find hope and healing for the individuals who are willing to put in the work of progressing toward physical, emotional, and spiritual health. By using this book and, if you're fortunate enough, also spending time with the horses, we hope to learn how to lean more closely into the Holy Spirit and create lasting memories with Him.

## More Than Just FBEAP

FBEAP is woven throughout this book, but there are also insightful teachings from other authors and lessons that God has placed on my heart. The journey to healing can take many paths and is unique to each individual. I pray that your healing journey has a *lasting* impact on your life. As I share the teachings that have been placed on my heart, you may think, *These are a tad cheesy*. Well, it was done that way on purpose! This ADD brain of mine, with the addition of a tad bit of brain damage from a neurological brain infection, has to be cheesy so I can remember. Cheesy equals easy! So my prayer is you will be able to remember them like I have because they have a fun Western theme!

---

4        Davis and Anderson, *Gal-Up Hope Trail*, 8.

★ ★ ★

# *It's time for*

# Unit 1

## Say Howdy to the Holy Spirit!

# Unit 1

# Say Howdy to the Holy Spirit!

Do you ever start the day with the best intentions of spending time in the Bible, only to get distracted? Maybe you pick up your phone to open your Bible app, only to see a social media notification or a text message. Before you know it, thirty minutes have passed, and you're still in bed without having spent any time with God. Just me? I didn't think so. In today's world, the Enemy is after our undivided attention. What better way to achieve that than by keeping us constantly distracted?

Another trick of the Enemy is to keep us busy. When you're running around everywhere, you come home exhausted and craving relaxation. Often, that downtime comes from technology. Too much busyness and screen time hijack us from what truly matters: our relationship with the Lord, our marriages, our families, and our self-care.

I am going to be completely vulnerable throughout this book because vulnerability can lead to truth and growth. I must admit that the Holy Spirit has deeply convicted me about how my daily habits pulled me further away from Him instead of drawing me closer. I have been on a journey of checking in with the Holy Spirit daily, and it has been life-changing!

In moments of stillness, we can hear Him speak to us through His Word and through heartfelt questions. Digging deep with Him through daily Bible reading and prayer time is essential. The Holy Spirit is the best riding partner we can have, but we will miss out on that nugget of truth if we don't make time to truly be with Him. Have you ever heard that voice convicting you about something in your life? If you are a follower of Jesus, then your Christian walk will lead onto trails that simply aren't followed by many of the other riders around you. Remember that God the Father, God the Son, and the Holy Spirit aren't just trying to point out the wrong paths that you have taken. That same voice—the one that you'll hear when you are seeking—doesn't just want to shine a light on your problems or mistakes; it desires to build you up, guide your life, and offer you a comfort that nobody else can provide!

## The HOWDY

I mentioned that you may hear the Holy Spirit speak to you in moments of stillness, but He may also gently guide you and your thoughts throughout the mundane tasks that you do each day. I feel so blessed that God spoke to me about this acronym one day while I was in the shower. He inspired me to use the word *HOWDY* as a way to check in with the Holy Spirit every day. By taking the time to do this, we will draw closer to Him and create a connection. What a simple and fun reminder; each day, we can ask ourselves, "Did I say howdy to the Holy Spirit today?"

**H** HOLY SPIRIT TIME! TAKE TIME TO BE STILL, PRAY, AND LISTEN.

**O** OBSERVE AND WRITE WHAT YOU ARE HEARING AND FEELING.

*"Howdy, Holy Spirit..."*

**W** WHAT DOES GOD'S WORD SAY? READ AND REFLECT ON SCRIPTURE.

**D** DISCOVER (ASK, SEEK, AND WRITE) WHAT THE HOLY SPIRIT HAS FOR YOU TO DO TODAY!

**Y** YES! YOU CAN DO WHAT HE LEADS YOU TO ACCOMPLISH!

*Don't forget to give prayer requests and praises!*

The best habit we can have is checking in daily with the Holy Spirit! I actually check in with the Holy Spirit each morning and evening—you may need to up your check-ins to twice a day as well. Are you struggling? Use a HOWDY to help you get connected to God!

★ ★ ★

# It's time for an
# Introduction
# of an
## FBEAP Philosophy

## It's Time to Introduce the
## First FBEAP – Foundational Principle:

# Pressure/Pain

First, I want to express how proud I am of you today! You have already shown an incredible display of facing pressure and pain just by being part of this study. You were presented with a choice (pressure) to participate or not, and you decided to move forward (into pain/ discomfort) for the purpose of healing and hope!

One of the six FBEAP philosophies is Pressure/Pain. In this philosophy, we observe how our equine partners respond physically and emotionally to pressure and pain, which in turn gives us insight into our responses. Do we recognize when we are feeling pressure versus pain? Are we responding in a healthy way? The horses, along with the guidance of the Holy Spirit, can help us learn how to evaluate and respond to the world around us.[5]

Horses exemplify a profound lesson from Jesus in their response to pressure. When faced with discomfort, they instinctively move forward; they embrace the challenge in order to find a resolution.[6] Jesus also confronted His struggles with courage and grace. He did not shy away from the pressures of life but felt them deeply and chose to move forward, even into pain, to fulfill His divine purpose. As He said, "Father, if you are willing, take this cup from me; yet not my will, but yours be done" (Luke 22:42 NIV). Jesus saw the pain of crucifixion that was coming, and while He asked His Father for relief, He ultimately pushed into the pressure and pain. His journey to the cross is a powerful reminder of His willingness to face hardship for our sake; it reflects a deep compassion and commitment to the greater good and the necessity to reconcile humanity with Creator.

I understand that this explanation may be difficult to grasp. I can relate. My battle with neurological Lyme disease has left me with some challenges, so I need easy-to-understand explanations. That's why I've included detailed illustrations throughout this book to help us all understand!

Now let's turn to the next page so I can explain Pressure/Pain in more detail for you.

---

5      Davis, *Foundations*, 22, 24.
6      Davis and Anderson, *Gal-Up Hope Trail*, 15.

## Pressure builds.

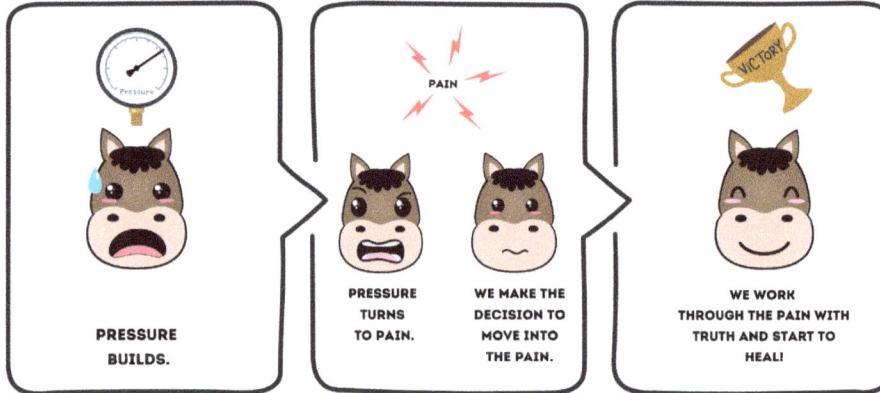

### PRESSURE

This includes our thoughts or actions or even other people's actions or opinions that we allow to remain or have to decide to deal with. Pressure turns to pain. We make the decision to move into the pain.

### PAIN/DISCOMFORT

Not dealing with pressure has become painful, and we start to believe lies. Also, the only way forward is to step into the pain. We work through the pain with truth and start to heal!

### TRUTH

We move forward into the pain with God's truth so we can heal.

As I mentioned earlier in this study, Our Healing Farm has received certification as an FBEAP facilitator through Unbridled™. Pressure/Pain is one of the principles taught through this program. You can learn more about this process through pressure building, pain, discomfort, and eventual healing in Elaine Davis's *Foundations* workbook when you get certified.[8]

### EXAMPLE OF PRESSURE/PAIN

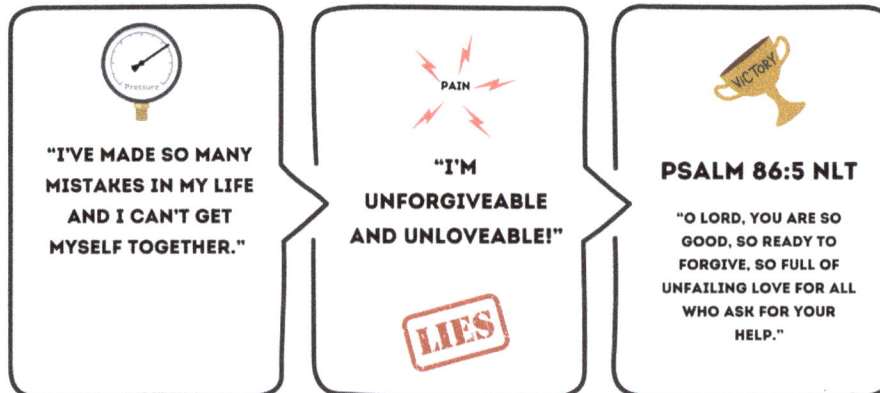

"I'VE MADE SO MANY MISTAKES IN MY LIFE AND I CAN'T GET MYSELF TOGETHER."

"I'M UNFORGIVEABLE AND UNLOVEABLE!"

LIES

**PSALM 86:5 NLT**

"O LORD, YOU ARE SO GOOD, SO READY TO FORGIVE, SO FULL OF UNFAILING LOVE FOR ALL WHO ASK FOR YOUR HELP."

---

7       Davis and Anderson, *Gal-Up Hope Trail*, 15.
8       Davis, *Foundations*, 24.
9       Davis and Anderson, *Gal-Up Hope Trail*, 13.

## It's Time to Introduce
## Another FBEAP – Foundational Principle:

# Confrontation

I want to introduce you to the next philosophy in FBEAP: Confrontation. This word can stir up anxiety in many of us, especially for recovering people-pleasers like me. I dreaded confrontation so much that I avoided it at all costs. Unfortunately, in avoiding the discomfort of confrontation, I ended up feeling unwell. I cared deeply about what others thought and never wanted to disappoint anyone; while I strived to please others, I allowed people to walk all over me constantly.

My journey as a people-pleaser began in childhood, rooted in some trauma. Once I realized this tendency wasn't serving me well, I knew I had to confront my issues instead of letting them fester. That's when I began to heal.

I'm highlighting confrontation this week because we can face anything with the Holy Spirit as our incredible riding partner. For those of you who are fortunate enough to work with us at Our Healing Farm, this week is a perfect opportunity to address confrontation as you work with the horses to identify difficult emotions. Instead of shying away from these feelings, I encourage you to confront them head-on.

Remember, we must confront pressure and pain to achieve victory. We are strong and capable with the Holy Spirit by our side!

| ANGER | → | PEACE |
| ABUSE | → | HOPE |
| FEAR | → | STRENGTH |
| PAIN | → | FREEDOM |

CONFRONTING TOUGH SITUATIONS WITH JESUS BESIDE US KNOWING WE ARE NOT ALONE

## Journey Forward Toward Healing

I like to think of confrontation in the way illustrated in the example above. Life is like a continuous trail ride, and when we choose to give our lives to Jesus, we gain a riding partner in the Holy Spirit. How blessed we are to have the option to let the Holy Spirit guide us along our life path. With Him by our side, we can confront challenging situations as we move forward.

Throughout the Bible, we see Jesus repeatedly confront situations head-on; just think of His conversations with the Pharisees. Horses demonstrate similar behavior; when a horse has an issue with another horse, it doesn't dwell on it for a week while ignoring the other horse. Instead, it addresses the issue right away, allowing the herd to function in a healthy way. This is essential for their survival.[10] For example, certain horses like their personal space while eating and resting; some are more apt to want to be in everyone's space. The horses who want personal space don't wait to tell the nosy horses later how annoyed they are; they handle the situation right away. Horses will tell the horse that's annoying them to back out of their space, usually by nipping or a swift kick. The issue gets resolved and the herd moves on. When you confront difficult emotions with the Holy Spirit as a guide, He can make the process just as manageable.

---

10    Davis, *Foundations*, 23.

# It's time for some
# Unit 1
## Check-Ins

# My Holy Spirit Experience

There was a very challenging time in my healing journey from neurological Lyme disease that became extremely dark for me. When we began treating the Lyme bacteria, it was a torturous experience. The doctor warned me that when the bacteria die, they put off toxic gases, and that I should be prepared for a dark experience. He wasn't wrong. My quality of life had already spiraled down, but then came blurry vision, memory loss, brain fog, insomnia, joint aches, facial tics, seizures, tremors, and debilitating fatigue. Even holding up my toothbrush felt like I was running a marathon. I couldn't drive, and I had to be monitored while bathing. Most days, I could hardly walk without feeling like I was going to pass out. My role as a mother reversed as my oldest child had to help care for me. I couldn't be the kind of wife Blake needed. I had been anointed with oil and prayed over, and we all prayed against spiritual warfare. But there was no relief. I didn't understand why God still wanted me to be in the midst of that pain and wouldn't heal me. I felt alone and hopeless. I wanted to be there to see my kids grow up, but at the same time, I felt my family deserved better. I even prayed for God to take me home. That may sound extreme, but that is how I felt.

One day, I decided to walk out toward the back of our property. That walk left me feeling fatigued and dizzy, so I sat on a log. As I looked around, our big barn caught my attention. That's when I thought to myself that I should walk off the top story to end all my pain. As I shook my head to regain my grip on reality, I realized that I probably wouldn't even die; I'd end up in a vegetative state and worse off than I was at that moment.

It was then that I cried out to God to express to Him how I was doing everything right, but these dark thoughts still plagued me. I sobbed and sobbed.

At that moment, I felt a *Presence* come around me and heard inside my mind a voice saying, "Melissa, this is physical. I need you to fight. Keep going and fight for your family. One day, this will all have a purpose."

I was in awe of the feeling that washed over my body. The Holy Spirit saved my life that day and gave me the power to keep fighting.

It was on that day, after that encounter, that I knew the only thing that could get me through this nightmare was God. I felt prompted to take a picture that day—the day I decided to fight and keep living.

I share that vulnerable story not to scare you, but to encourage you. There is nothing too big for God. He is in control and knows what He is doing. It's through taking the time to grow closer to Him that we feel His presence the most. I say this from the deepest part of my heart: Don't wait until you're facing a life-or-death situation or extreme trial to seek that closeness. It's not a question of whether you will face trials, but when. Just think of what Jesus said to His disciples! "I have told you these things, so that in me you may have peace. In this world you will have trouble. But take heart! I have overcome the world" (John 16:33 NIV). Seek a life led by the Holy Spirit now so that when trials come your way, you are strong enough to endure and have the power *from God* to get through them.

## Check-In and Homework Time

1. Reflect on a time when you were absolutely certain that God helped you through a difficult experience. Write about it below:

2. Take a moment to write a sentence of gratitude to the Lord for getting you through that time.

It's okay if you can't think of a time—don't be discouraged. Healing is a journey that takes time; this is not a race. You're doing great!

## Being Still

Read these Bible verses and reflect on them:

"Be still, and know that I am God!
   I will be honored by every nation.
   I will be honored throughout the world" (Psalm 46:10).

"Be still in the presence of the Lord,
   and wait patiently for him to act.
Don't worry about evil people who prosper
   or fret about their wicked schemes" (Psalm 37:7).

"When Jesus woke up, he rebuked the wind and said to the waves, 'Silence! Be still!' Suddenly the wind stopped, and there was a great calm" (Mark 4:39).

"The Lord will fight for you; you need only to be still" (Exodus 14:14 NIV).

"Don't sin by letting anger control you.
   Think about it overnight and remain silent" (Psalm 4:4).

"Now, O sword of the Lord,
   when will you be at rest again?
Go back into your sheath;
   rest and be still" (Jeremiah 47:6).

3. Keep in mind that these are just a few of the verses in the Bible that instruct us to be still. Why do you think the Bible tells us to be still so many times?

4. How are you when it comes time to be still? Is it an easy exercise for you, or quite difficult?

I don't know about you, but I hear God most clearly when I find a quiet place and still my mind. God understands that He needs our undivided attention to nurture our relationship with Him. Some of my most profound *Be Still* moments happen in the shower! Why? I think it's because my mind becomes calm and relaxed without distractions. Is this just me, or have others experienced this too? I don't know, but I'm grateful that He speaks to me wherever He chooses. I have had some life-giving things spoken to me in the shower . . . just like the HOWDY acronym!

5. What can you do to become better at being still?

# Checking In on FBEAP – Foundational Principle: Confrontation

Earlier in this unit, I explained the importance of confrontation, especially when it is done through the power of God the Father, Jesus, and the Holy Spirit. Now that we're in a check-in spot, I have a few questions for you.

1. How do you feel about confronting things in your life?

2. Would you say you accomplish confrontation in a healthy or unhealthy way?

3. Do you believe you have the best riding partner by always having the Holy Spirit with you?

4. Do you struggle with remembering God is in control?

When it comes to confrontation, you must remember that you cannot control the outcome; you can only control your own actions, not the actions of others. The most important thing that you and I can do is trust that God has a plan for us. Therefore, when you face your wounds—whether they are internal or related to your relationships with others—you can have faith that He knows what is best for you.

However, acknowledging your lack of control over a confrontation's outcome does not mean you can simply avoid it altogether. If you avoid confrontation out of fear, you are not allowing (or even inviting) God to resolve the issues. I understand that confrontation can be difficult, but it's worth the journey forward rather than remaining stuck.

## Our Riding Partner

Do you remember reading that "The Holy Spirit is the best riding partner we can have" in the beginning of unit one? With that same thought in the forefront of your mind, take some time to dig into the Word. Look up and write out these Bible verses. Be still and reflect on them.

| John 14:16–17 | |
| --- | --- |
| Romans 15:13 | |
| John 16:13 | |
| Galatians 5:25 | |

1. What stands out most to you about these verses?

2. How would you rate your closeness to the Holy Spirit (1 being poor and 5 being excellent)?

As I have already shared, I love to think of the Holy Spirit as the best riding partner we can have on this journey through life. As you read in those verses, He wants to be close to us. Since God has granted us free will, it is our choice whether or not we allow Him to be a part of our lives.

3. What would you say gets in the way the most with you spending daily time with God?

4. Think of one change you can make to spend more time with Him and try it out!

As you embark on your journey to listen for God's voice, it is essential to be still and carefully discern what you hear. Ensure that it resonates with the wisdom found in Scripture and embodies the essence of God's nature—loving, just, and compassionate. By making this practice a regular habit, you will gradually sharpen your sensitivity to His voice.

When you set aside time to read your Bible, worship God, and intercede for loved ones and yourself in prayer, you may start to hear that "still small voice" that Elijah heard (1 Kings 19:12–13 KJV).

At that point, you may start to ask yourself another question.

## Howdy, Partner! Listen Closely.

Have you ever felt confused as to what voice you are hearing? This confusion is not necessarily a bad place to be. The fact that you are even questioning the thoughts and voices around you can lead you to deeper understandings of yourself and of God.

Here are some things to keep in mind while you are determining just where the voice or thought may be coming from.[11]

---

11      Janet Eriksson, "Three Voices – Yours, The Enemy's, and God's," *Adventures with God* (blog), published January 22, 2019, https://adventureswithgod.blog/2019/01/22/three-voices-yours-the-enemy-and-god/.

# Discerning God's Voice

## God's Voice:

God's voice is gentle, comforting, and calming. It stills and guides you. When He convicts, it isn't a condemning voice, but soft. God's voice can be heard in Scripture, just as Paul said to Timothy when he wrote, "All Scripture is God-breathed and is useful for teaching, rebuking, correcting and training in righteousness" (2 Timothy 3:16 NIV).

## The Voice of Darkness:

The Enemy's voice instills worry, fear, shame, and confusion. His voice feels condemning and pushy through the lies that lead us away from God's nature of truth. Jesus explained Satan's voice clearly when He said, "When he lies, he speaks his native language, for he is a liar and the father of lies" (John 8:44 NIV). It's our job to lasso the bull (thought) and bring God's truth to it. If it doesn't align with Scripture, then we know it isn't from the Lord.

## Our Own Inner Voice:

Our voices can feel loud as well. Because of this, you must decipher whether your feelings are rooted in God's truth. Does the voice feel condemning? Does it feel loud or soft? Does it feel confusing? Those are all good questions you can ask yourself to lasso the truth!

★ ★ ★

We are almost ready to wrap up unit one! Friend, saying, "Howdy, Holy Spirit" is just the beginning of your journey to healing. Before you can fully step into these moments with the third Person of the Trinity, you may need to look at what the Bible says about the Holy Spirit and the voices all around you.

Read these Bible verses below:

> "But the Advocate, the Holy Spirit, whom the Father will send in my name, will teach you all things and will remind you of everything I have said to you" (John 14:26 NIV).

> "My sheep listen to my voice; I know them, and they follow me" (John 10:27).

> "Your own ears will hear him. Right behind you a voice will say, 'This is the way you should go,' whether to the right or to the left" (Isaiah 30:21).

> "Behold, I stand at the door and knock. If anyone hears my voice and opens the door, I will come in to him and eat with him, and he with me" (Revelation 3:20 ESV).

Now that you've read these four verses, take some time to meditate on them.

1. What speaks to you most in those verses?

2. Do you believe the Holy Spirit speaks to us and guides us?

3. If you **do** believe that the Holy Spirit speaks to us and guides us, then when do you hear Him best?

Part of the basis for FBEAP philosophies hinge on the herd mentality. Think about it—just as people and horses were created to be in community, so also is God in community through the Trinity.

★ ★ ★

# Even Jesus Needed the Holy Spirit!

Read Luke 4:1–14 and summarize what you have read below.

1. How did Jesus get through the hardship of being tempted in the wilderness?

If even Jesus, the Son of God, had to rely heavily on the Holy Spirit to guide Him through the wilderness and on His journey to the cross, why do we allow the world to make us think we can do things on our own? I believe the reality is that we cannot. We may manage for a while, but eventually our bodies, souls, and spirits begin to struggle.

Let's take celebrities as an example. Our society often puts celebrities up on pedestals. Their lives seem to be magical and without any real concerns! They may have all the money and resources in the world, yet many end up facing issues like drug abuse, depression, and broken relationships. Despite the worldly resources that they have an abundance of, there is still a real need for their spiritual needs. Nothing in this world can provide us with lasting love, strength, or power like God can. Period.

2. What are some things you like to control instead of acknowledging God's control and sovereignty?

3. Do you need to be better about relying on God?

★ ★ ★

## Checking In on FBEAP – Foundational Principle: Pressure/Pain

Do you remember what we learned about the FBEAP regarding Pressure/Pain? If not, now is a good time to look back at those explanations. Once you have the philosophy solidified in your mind, you can analyze just how well you do with Pressure/Pain in your everyday life.

1.  In your life, what represents pressure?

2. Likewise, what represents pain (discomfort)?

3. Are you ready to move forward into the pain toward healing and hope through truth?

★ ★ ★

# Prayers and Praises

★ ★ ★

# *It's time for*
# Unit 2
## Say Howdy to Herd Life!

## Unit 2

# Say Howdy to Herd Life!

While unit one focused on the role of and our connection to the Holy Spirit, this section will dive deeper into the need for relationships. Having the Holy Spirit is essential for healing, but being part of a community, or herd, is a crucial second aspect.

Some of you may already be well aware of how important circles of friends and family are, but I first learned about functioning as a herd at a certification clinic I attended with Unbridled™, led by Elaine Davis. It was emphasized that God did not create us to live in isolation; rather, we are meant to live with a community mindset, much like a horse herd.

In my quest to understand how to maintain a healthy herd, I have also gained valuable insights from Dr. Karl D. Lehman. In his books *The Immanuel Approach* and *Outsmarting Yourself*, Lehman introduced the concept of relational circuits, which has been incredibly helpful to me in receiving healing in my life. Relational circuits are essential because when these circuits in our brain are activated, we genuinely feel glad to be with a person or spend time with God, and they, in turn, are glad to be with us.

Friend, if you really want to create a healthy herd to surround yourself with, then you may need to commit to seeking out books or other resources that focus on healthy relationships. I will reference several books in the back of this study—ones that have added both to the creation of Our Healing Farm as well as to the compilation of this study that you are reading right now. When I share information in this book, whether from FBEAP industry experts like Elaine Davis or other specialists, know that these are just snippets of their teachings. To further transform your life, I encourage you to purchase and read the books listed in my Resources section. You will not be disappointed by the value that reading and applying their teachings will add to your life.

For right now though, let's focus back in on the concept of a herd life. In our exploration of how to cultivate a healthy herd and closer relationship with the Holy Spirit, we will discuss concepts such as levels of maturity, relational circuits, relationship bonds, spurring each other on, and FBEAP's Relationship Zones.

Let's start with levels of maturity first!

## Levels of Maturity

In this section, we'll saddle up and ride through the different stages of maturity—using the world of horseback riding as our guide. We will compare maturity levels to the stages of learning to ride a horse. I want to note that this section is inspired by the book *Living From the Heart Jesus Gave You,* which categorizes maturity levels into five distinct groups: Infant, Child, Adult, Parent, and Elder. The book emphasizes the importance of understanding these maturity levels in a way that encourages reflection on personal growth and recognition of development in others, ultimately promoting healthier relationships.[12]

## Why Some Adults Remain in Childlike States

Understanding maturity is an interesting topic. I have noticed in my experiences that some adults still behave in childlike ways. Many of us can relate to this and may even see it in ourselves at times.

In the book *Living From the Heart Jesus Gave You,* the authors explain that in the first three years of life, children must experience bonding and joy to create emotional pathways for returning to joy, which are developed through parental attentiveness. Without this connection, children may struggle to manage their emotions. If infants lack critical attention from caregivers, they fail to form essential emotional pathways, and this will result in immature adult behaviors. They might not have developed the pathway to regulate their emotions.[13]

Fortunately, we can still cultivate our joy centers throughout life through relationships with God and others. When our joy centers are filled, we can begin to heal from trauma and find our way back to joy.[14]

Let's take a closer look at the different stages of maturity and how God wants us to understand them.

---

12    James Friesen et. al, *Living From the Heart Jesus Gave You* (Shepherd's House, 2016), 36–46.
13    Friesen, *Living From the Heart Jesus Gave You,* 74–81.
14    Friesen, *Living From the Heart Jesus Gave You,* 33–35.

# Understanding Maturity

### Starting in the Saddle: The Infant Stage

Learning to ride a horse for beginners is much like infancy—everything feels new and overwhelming, requiring guidance from trainers or parents. Riders rely on support as they navigate balance and emotions, much like infants, who depend entirely on caregivers for safety and love. Trust is essential for growth; just as babies need to believe they will be caught if they fall, beginner riders must trust their trainers and horses.

**0-3 YEARS OLD**

Infants lacking the nurturing they need may carry those emotional gaps into adulthood, functioning like needy, self-doubting individuals who cannot take any form of criticism. They might struggle to ask for help or form supportive relationships, appearing competent but stuck in earlier stages of emotional development,[15] similar to a rider who never fully takes the reins.

## Wrangling Youth: The Child Stage

Once infants start to express their needs, they move into the child stage. This is when they begin learning to care for themselves and grow more independent.[16] Like young riders learning to steer and ride, children explore their world with curiosity. They begin to talk about their needs, try new things, face challenges, discover their gifts, and learn their place in the world.[17]

Just like learning to ride a horse takes practice and patience, children grow through trial and error. They will feel both joy and frustration. Mistakes—like falling off a horse or doing the wrong thing—are part of the learning process.

**4-12 YEARS OLD**

Children need love and support during this stage. Parents should give unconditional love, just like God loves us—not based on

---

15    Friesen, *Living From the Heart Jesus Gave You*, 36–38.
16    Friesen, *Living From the Heart Jesus Gave You*, 38–39.
17    Friesen, *Living From the Heart Jesus Gave You*, 38–39.

success or behavior, but simply because the child is valuable.[18] This steady love helps children feel safe and confident.

As they grow, kids start to feel satisfaction from their accomplishments[19]—like new riders brushing the horse or putting on the saddle by themselves. These moments build confidence and teach responsibility. With love and support, children begin to understand who they are and how to care for themselves.

However, when adults did not receive adequate care and emotional support as children, they may carry childlike tendencies into adulthood. These unresolved needs and struggles can manifest as difficulty managing emotions and developing selfish behaviors that harm their relationships.[20]

## Steady in the Saddle: The Adult Stage

**13 YEARS OLD TO THE BIRTH OF THE FIRST CHILD**

Adulthood is when we grow beyond thinking only of ourselves and start truly caring for others. We begin to give back to our families and communities in meaningful ways. With God's help, we learn to stay stable during hard times, hold on to truth, and return to joy, even when life is tough.[21]

This stage is like the rider who has learned the basics and now rides with confidence—able to saddle the horse, warm up, manage different gaits, and respond to the horse naturally. In the same way, a mature adult moves through life with purpose and direction.

Adults no longer need constant approval from others. Instead, they live from the wisdom and strength God has built in them. Maturity—both in riding and in life—is about finding balance, staying steady, and being committed to growing, loving others, and walking closely with God.

---

18    Friesen, *Living From the Heart Jesus Gave You*, 38.
19    Friesen, *Living From the Heart Jesus Gave You*, 39.
20    Friesen, *Living From the Heart Jesus Gave You*, 39.
21    Friesen, *Living From the Heart Jesus Gave You*, 39.

## Guiding the Herd: The Parent Stage

As riders grow more skilled, they often take on new roles—teaching younger students, caring for multiple horses, or training inexperienced ones. Their focus shifts from personal growth to supporting others, offering wisdom, patience, and protection as guides. This shift mirrors the journey of parenting, where maturity involves selfless care, emotional guidance, and a willingness to learn and grow alongside others. Having children alone doesn't guarantee you achieve this level of maturity; it comes from sacrificing without resentment or expectation, recognizing one's limitations, and embracing support from wise mentors.[22] Just as mature riders share their knowledge to help the next generation build a strong foundation, mature parents balance protection and joy, helping their children navigate emotions and discover resilience. In both roles, entitlement has no place—only humility, service, and the desire to nurture growth.[23]

**FROM THE BIRTH OF THE FIRST CHILD TO WHEN THE YOUNGEST CHILD IS GROWN**

## The Faithful Trail Boss: The Elder Stage

At the highest level of horsemanship, the rider no longer needs to prove anything. They ride not for fame or winning but to enjoy a deep connection with their horse, given by God. They may ride less often but with more care and attention. They naturally understand the horse's feelings and needs, as if led by God's wisdom. Often, they become gentle helpers or teachers, supporting others without being in the spotlight.

This stage of horsemanship mirrors the role of an elder in life. Not everyone reaches this level of maturity, but once your children are grown, you may attain the status of elder. This blessing allows you to help others navigate difficult situations while keeping joy and peace.[24] Like the seasoned rider, you become a strong support within your family and

**FROM WHEN THE YOUNGEST CHILD IS GROWN THROUGH THE REST OF LIFE**

22      Friesen, *Living From the Heart Jesus Gave You,* 41.
23      Friesen, *Living From the Heart Jesus Gave You,* 41.
24      Friesen, *Living From the Heart Jesus Gave You,* 41–42.

community, walking alongside others with patience and care. You have a solid foundation with God that keeps you steady in the hardest times.[25] You understand that your ministry to people continues throughout your life—being older doesn't mean you stop helping others. You also learn to guide your older children with respect and love rather than bossing them around.

Elders, like trusted trail bosses and master riders, draw from a lifetime of experience and offer God's wisdom, sound presence, and calm resilience. Able to handle criticism with grace, they become trusted mentors, guiding the community with insight and compassion.[26] Their presence is a grounding force, reminding us that true mastery isn't about doing more—it's about becoming more: more present, more understanding, and more in tune with God's plan.

Let's take a look at some fictional characters that I have created to give an example of understanding levels of maturity:

**First, let me introduce you to Hank,** a sixty-five-year-old cowboy from southern Texas who was very well cared for by his parents. He had a wonderful childhood. In the infant stage, he was showered with affection, but his parents also knew when he needed space. Hank was taught to face life's challenges by wise mentors. His parents were humble enough to seek help when necessary, allowing him to excel.

During his child stage, which spans from ages four through twelve, Hank learned to communicate, tackle challenges, recognize his talents, and understand his place in the world.

When he entered the adult stage, which is from age thirteen to the birth of a person's first child, Hank exhibited remarkable maturity. He was capable of caring for others, finding stability in tough situations, and experiencing joy. Hank loved contributing to his community, embracing the truth that God offers, and living a fulfilling life.

It's no surprise that Hank smoothly transitioned into the parent stage. But not every individual reaches this stage. Hank became an incredible father, helping his children navigate

---

25      Friesen, *Living From the Heart Jesus Gave You*, 41.
26      Friesen, *Living From the Heart Jesus Gave You*, 42.

difficult emotions and rediscover joy. Additionally, he served as a supportive mentor to his wife and friends. As a mature parent, Hank understood that he couldn't meet every need independently and was open to guidance from wise adults.

Once all of Hank's children were grown, he reached the final stage of maturity—the elder stage—an achievement many never attain. In this phase, Hank could help others navigate challenging situations while maintaining a sense of joy. He became a strong support within his family and community, walking alongside others in their struggles. His solid foundation in his faith helped him remain stable in the most challenging circumstances. Hank understood that his ministry to others continued throughout his life; his older age did not mean he was finished helping those around him. He also knew how to guide his older children rather than simply instruct them.

Hank may seem almost too good to be true—a picture-perfect individual. Hank was fortunate; his upbringing by mature parents was truly a gift. They prepared him to live a joy-filled life and showed him how to find the strength to handle difficulties.

As I reflect on Hank's fictional life, I find myself envious. Can you imagine? I didn't have that luxury, and I suspect many of you reading this may feel the same way. So let's meet our next character, Hank's wife:

**Bonnie was the fifth-born child in her family,** born less than a year after her older brother. Her mother, Loretta, had very little support from her husband, who was emotionally detached due to his traumatic past and had turned to alcohol to cope. Additionally, Loretta lost her mother at a young age and, into adulthood, had an estranged relationship with her father. This situation limited the help Loretta could receive to care for her kids; in turn, this affected Bonnie.

As a baby, Bonnie struggled to get attention due to the close age gap with her brother. By age eight, she had three younger siblings. There was only so much of Loretta to go around. Bonnie had an inattentive alcoholic father and an overly stressed mother. Although Loretta did provide care, affection was limited, which impacted the development of Bonnie's brain pathways.

As Bonnie entered childhood, the weight of her father's alcoholism grew heavier, coinciding with the toxicity of

her parents' marriage. To keep peace, Bonnie became a people-pleaser, trying to be an easy child. This was a challenging act to maintain. Eventually, she began seeking validation from boys to fill the emotional void she experienced at home.

Blessings smiled upon Bonnie when she met Hank, who introduced her to God, bringing her a calmer and more joyful world. However, Bonnie was still stunted in her maturity level (infant-child), responding to even small triggers with extreme agitation. When she became a parent, Bonnie faced overwhelming challenges. She struggled to provide the affection and patience her children needed as she had rarely experienced these feelings from her parents. Isolation, outbursts, and avoidance became her coping mechanisms, leaving Hank with a heavy burden. Bonnie's lingering infantile/childlike immaturity was affecting their children and her marriage.

Fortunately, God placed many mature individuals in Bonnie's life who were committed to her growth. Also, as Bonnie grew closer to the Lord, God revealed the concept of immaturity to her, and she became determined to address her traumatic past and eventually developed into the person God intended her to be.

Your story may differ from Bonnie's, and your challenges might stem from various circumstances. Perhaps you spent time in the foster care system or were raised in a really large family where there wasn't enough parental time to give you the attention you needed. It's possible that your parents were stuck in immaturity and unable to meet your needs. I empathize with your situation. The good news is that you can still develop your joy center now. All hope is not lost!

## Examples of Infantile and Childlike Maturity

The following images may seem juvenile or even silly, but learning about levels of maturity allows you to examine your behavior as well as that of others in your herd. As I said earlier, when we strive to grow, it allows us to improve ourselves and our herds!

I have a hard time controlling my emotions. Sometimes this may even mimic a tantrum.

I care more about my needs than others.

I pout when I don't get my way.

**Stuck** in Infantile & Childlike **MATURITY**

I have a need to always be right.

When I don't get my way, I punish those who actually love me by pulling away.

## Can You Improve Your Maturity?

Now that you have learned about maturity levels through our fictional characters (Hank and Bonnie), I encourage you to assess where you stand so you can grow! Have you matured into an adult, parent, or elder? If not, do you have a herd that can push you through the pressure that comes with change? Remember how important our herds are when it comes to working through healing, whether from physical, emotional, or spiritual ailments. Learning about how we and others interact within communities is an integral step that we believe in at Our Healing Farm.

Remember, these examples of childlike maturity levels are also discussed in greater detail in Dr. Friesen's writing —this is another resource that you can use in your own healing journey.[27]

The next lesson I have for you is on relational circuits. Let's ride on over to the next topic!

## Relational Circuits Within Yourself and Your Herd

Do you understand what it means to have a relational connection? It means that a person—or God—is genuinely glad to be with you.[28]

Have you ever spoken to someone and noticed that their eyes and mind seem to be elsewhere? It's clear they are distracted and not fully engaged. You might even know the reason behind their disconnection, especially if you are connected to the issue affecting them. Our brains are wired with circuits that help us connect with others and nurture our relationship with God. To function at our best, these circuits need to be activated, which means we must be connected to the person we are interacting with or to God.

However, as Dr. Lehman teaches, our circuits can become inactive when we are triggered by something.[29] This could be a situation that annoys, upsets, or worries us. These emotions can cause our circuits to shut down. Understanding these relational circuits is crucial for maintaining a healthy self and community. By becoming aware of them, we can recognize when we need to engage in exercises to reconnect and get our circuits firing again.

Personally, I find that when I'm stressed or have a lot going on, my ability to focus turns off as well. It can be discouraging when we feel that someone isn't paying attention to us. However, upon reflection, we may realize that we also weren't fully engaged in the moment. I struggle with this myself, especially since I experienced brain damage that affected my multitasking ability. If my mind is elsewhere, I find it hard to connect with others. I often feel bad about this. To improve my connections with my family, I need to stop, center my thoughts, and set aside all distractions.

Getting to a place where you're not triggered is essential for reactivating your brain circuits. As Dr. Lehman explains, it is possible to turn relational circuits on.[30] There are four helpful

---

27      Friesen, *Living From the Heart Jesus Gave You*, 36–46.
28      Karl Lehman, *The Immanuel Approach: For Emotional Healing and for Life* (Immanuel Publishing, 2024), 1217, 1234–1238.
29      Karl Lehman, *Outsmarting Yourself: Catching Your Past Invading the Present and What to Do About It* (This Joy! Books, 2011), 209, 211–13.
30      Lehman, *Outsmarting Yourself*, 217–51.

ways to power them back on:

1. Attuning to someone or to God, if you can

2. Calming your body

3. Expressing gratitude to the Lord

4. Accessing humor

We will explore how to do these more in the homework assignments. At Our Healing Farm, I like to refer to this process as resetting the brain!

## Discern Whether Relational Circuits Are Off or On

### When they are *off*, we may experience:

- My mind is stuck in upset.
- I do not desire to attune and connect to others.
- I'm annoyed or worried instead of listening.
- I want the person or problem just to leave.
- I have no patience.
- I feel like running away and isolating.
- I go into fix-it mode.
- I'm feeling like judging, fighting, and arguing.
- I'm distracted by my own issues and stress.
- I'm building my case against them.

**When they are *on*, we may experience:**

- I'm joyful to be with this person.
- I actually want to attune to them.
- I want to make positive eye contact.
- I have a desire to solve the problem because the person is worth it.
- I can see they have a true heart, and they are not my enemy.
- I don't want to retreat.
- I can solve problems fairly with compassion.
- I see the importance in the person is worth me putting aside distractions.
- I feel like learning something from what is happening.[31]

God created us to connect with others and, in turn, desire connection for ourselves. To attune ourselves means to pay attention and listen when people speak to us. Attunement is important if we truly want to connect with others and the Lord.[32] To be able to attune, we have to have our relational circuits turned on.

Let's take a moment to review some of the terms that have come up in unit two as I've asked you to focus on *herd life*! You have read about the following topics:

- **Levels of Maturity**
- **Relational Circuits**
- **Attunement**

Do each of these make sense to you, and can you see how relevant they are to a herd or community?

I'm about to share another concept with you, and I want to be sure that you are right on track with me!

---

31    Lehman, *Outsmarting Yourself*, 211–13.
32    Lehman, *Outsmarting Yourself*, 181.

# Sound Attachments vs. Lame Attachments

Having secure relationships where we can share our experiences and make relational connections is vital to having a healthy herd. Let's take a look at what relationships based on soundness and lameness look like.[33]

**Sound attachments** are life-giving. The people who are truthful, loving, and engaged when you are with them truly make a difference. They support you through the ups and downs of life and genuinely want what is best for you. These are the kinds of individuals who encourage your success and happiness.

**Lame attachments** can remind me of a sly fox or a wolf in sheep's clothing as they are not always authentic. The person can be inconsistent or make you feel as though you're in a one-sided relationship. They may use fear, confusion, and manipulation to maintain the connection. Their engagement with you isn't always genuine; they can be self-absorbed, which leaves you feeling exhausted. Lameness can also be characterized by having an unbridled tongue and not being mindful of how they are treating someone they love. Lame attachments are not life-giving!

Those in the horse world know where I got the terms *sound* and *lame*. When a horse is lame, it means they are in pain and cannot perform to the best of their abilities due to an injury in their limb. They need help to recover, or sometimes it signifies the end of their life. On the other hand, the term *sound* indicates that the horse is healthy and ready to reach its full potential. I want you to think about it this way as we discuss relationships: *Lame* represents life-sucking, while *sound* embodies life-giving.

---

33    This section is adapted from Friesen, *Living From the Heart Jesus Gave You*, 69.

Building loving, sound attachments is essential for creating healthy and fulfilling connections that nurture both individuals. It's essential to remember that developing strong and meaningful relationships can be challenging, but the effort is truly worth it. Together, we can strive to cultivate connections that uplift us and enrich our lives. You are valuable, and you deserve the love and support that come from these deep connections.[34]

Merriam-Webster defines a spur as "a pointed device secured to a [horse] rider's heel,"[35] and it is used to encourage the horse to move forward.

Are you motivating people in a positive way, a negative way, or not at all? It's worthwhile to consider the fact that spurs can be a firm nudge to a horse as well. Sometimes the horses need this pressure to push them forward. This should echo back to the FBEAP principle of Pressure/Pain. Can you recognize when someone in your herd, or even you, needs a firm nudge to push forward? It's crucial to ensure that your loved ones feel seen and heard, and to do so in ways that respect their bodies, minds, and spirits.

Being part of a healthy herd also involves encouraging one another to grow closer to Jesus. Do you have daily time devoted to reading your Bible or praying? Do you know if those in your herd have that time as well? Look back at what a sound relationship offers. When you are encouraging your herd to seek Jesus, it will inevitably lead to personal growth and closeness within your relationship as well.

**You can't go wrong spurring people on!**

Spur

People on

Using positive

Recognition

---

34    Friesen, *Living From the Heart Jesus Gave You*, 59.
35    *Merriam-Webster*, s.v. "spur (*n.*)," accessed September 16, 2025, https://www.merriam-webster.com/dictionary/spur.

## What Do You Hang Your Hat On?

Have you ever encountered the idioms "hang your hat on" or "hang your hat with"? When people use these expressions, they indicate that they rely on something or someone they consider trustworthy and dependable.

But what if we *hang our hats* on the wrong things, or with the wrong people? What if we have invited in strongholds or toxic relationships, and they have become something we have truly begun to rely on?

The Bible teaches us about the armor of God. In Ephesians 6:11–13, Paul said to the people of Ephesus, "Put on the whole armor of God, that you may be able to stand against the schemes of the devil. For we do not wrestle against flesh and blood, but against the rulers, against the authorities, against the cosmic powers over this present darkness, against the spiritual forces of evil in the heavenly places. Therefore, take up the whole armor of God, that you may be able to withstand in the evil day, and having done all, to stand firm" (ESV).

## Give the Enemy the Boot!

This verse reveals a powerful truth: A spiritual realm is fighting against us, and we must put on the whole armor of God to give the Enemy the boot!

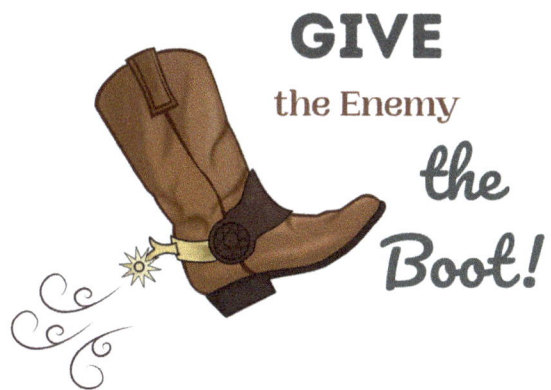

Do you think the Enemy wants you healed? I can wholeheartedly tell you he doesn't. If he can keep you comfortable in bondage, he will! Too many times, I have seen oppressed individuals who chose to stay in bondage rather than take authority (Luke 10:19) and pray against it. Healing is a choice and a lot of work. It is also one choice that nobody else can make for you.

Friend, I pray all the time against spiritual warfare attacking my life. I personally feel I have to stay on top of it regularly to thrive in this world we are living in.

## Hanging Your Hat on Strongholds

You may or may not be familiar with the term *stronghold*. If you look it up in the dictionary, you may read about a fortified structure. That sounds positive, right? Yet in Christian theology, strongholds usually have negative connotations. In this meaning, you can see where habits or sinful choices lead to deeper mental, emotional, or spiritual chains built by deception and repeated lies. This is not a new concept; Paul wrote about this thousands of years ago when he sent letters to the people of Corinth. As Paul and Timothy wrote, "We use God's mighty weapons, not worldly weapons, to knock down the strongholds of human reasoning and to destroy false arguments" (2 Corinthians 10:4–5). These citadels of doubt, fear, insecurity, or fleshly patterns hold us captive. When we *hang our hats on* them, we trust them as safe—even though they lead us away from truth and into captivity.

## No Hat on Strongholds, Only on God's Armor

To truly experience healing, you cannot hang your hat on any of these things:

- Broken identities
- Lies about your past
- Toxic people
- Beliefs built in darkness

Instead, hang your hat on God's unfailing truth, the armor He provides, His Word, and surround yourself with sound people. Stand firm, determined that you do deserve healing.

# It's time for an
# Introduction
# of an
## FBEAP Philosophy

## It's Time to Introduce
## Another FBEAP – Foundational Principle:

# Relationship Zones

**STOP ZONE**

**RELATE ZONE**

**MOTIVATED ZONE**

THIS IS THE MOMENT YOU WOULD USE A BRAKE PEDAL OR CALL OUT, "WHOA!"

THIS IS WHERE YOU CAN BE GUIDED BY GOD.

THIS IS WHERE YOU CAN BE ENERGIZED BY GOD.

[36]

In horse herds, the animals rely on each other and share a genuine sense of community. FBEAP taps into this relational tenet; this is what Relationship Zones are all about. Just as God created horses to be drawn into herds, He created people to thrive in community as well. A letter written thousands of years ago to Jews who had converted to Christianity says, "Let us think of ways to motivate one another to acts of love and good works. And let us not neglect our meeting together, as some people do, but encourage one another, especially now that the day of His return is drawing near" (Hebrews 10:24–25). This passage gives multiple points of insight: The words of encouragement that people needed not long after Jesus walked the earth are the same words of encouragement that you and I

---

36    Davis, *Foundations*, 28.

need today, and God desires His people to spur one another on! These verses highlight the importance of relationships, not only with God but also within a community. God never intended for us to go through life alone. The key to good relationships is making sure we are in healthy Relationship Zones with the Lord so we can have healthy relationships with others.

# It's time for some
# Unit 2
## Check-Ins

## Check-In and Homework Time

# Part One: Levels of Maturity

1. As you reflect on levels of maturity (pages 37–43), what thoughts arise regarding your own level of maturity?

2. The book of 1 Corinthians has several verses that speak directly to this idea of maturity. Read the two verses below; then write out what stands out to you or even which principle from FBEAP they relate to.

   "Yet when I am among mature believers, I do speak with words of wisdom, but not the kind of wisdom that belongs to this world or to the rulers of this world, who are soon forgotten" (1 Corinthians 2:6).

   "Dear brothers and sisters, don't be childish in your understanding of these things. Be innocent as babies when it comes to evil, but be mature in understanding matters of this kind" (1 Corinthians 14:20).

3. Look up Hebrews 5:11–14. Read and reflect on its truths below:

4. Do you want to be more mature in your spiritual life?

★ ★ ★

5. You've just read about spiritual maturity in the books of 1 Corinthians and Hebrews. Why do you think God taught us about the need for maturity?

6. Do you think you should ever stop maturing spiritually?

7. Finally, look up Psalm 92:14–15 and reflect below:

Friend, you will not be done growing spiritually until you pass away. Some of the most influential people who have helped me in my spiritual life are twenty to forty years older than I am! Imagine if they had decided they were done maturing in their twenties or thirties; I would have missed out on the wisdom they gained through their later years. That's why it's so important for spiritually mature individuals to come alongside less mature Christians. You may need to read that last sentence again! Did you notice that it did **not** say it's important for older individuals to mentor younger ones? Spiritual maturity isn't *necessarily* based on age alone but on the time, effort, and work of the Holy Spirit within a person's heart and mind. We need that relational connection with people who have sought the Lord and studied His Word!

As you assess the maturity levels, do you feel you are stuck or see the need to do the work to mature to the next level? The process of healing that leads to hope takes work! I pray that you take this call seriously. It would be much easier to live your life in a way that leaves you isolated and stuck in one place. Don't you think the Enemy wants nothing more than to keep us spiritually inhibited and immature? "Satan, who is the god of this world, has blinded the minds of those who don't believe. They are unable to see the glorious light of the Good News. They don't understand this message about the glory of Christ, who is the exact likeness of God" (2 Corinthians 4:4). I know that Satan and the spiritual forces that work with him want you and me to remain spiritually immature—this verse makes that clear too. Unfortunately, if we can remain spiritually immature, then he has us silenced and just where he wants us—stagnant!

Can you think of a person God has placed in your life who is spiritually mature and can help you grow in your own spiritual maturity? Take a moment to tell them how special they

are and that you recognize their maturity. This encouragement can help them continue growing in Christ.

Friend, unit two has placed a big emphasis on levels of maturity, both from references from *Living From the Heart Jesus Gave You* and from biblical perspectives. Our primary mission should be to become spiritually mature to the *highest* level possible so we can make the most significant impact for God while we are here on earth. If you feel that some buried trauma is blocking your growth in maturity, you are not alone. Stay committed to the healing journey; God will mend those wounds so you can reach your fullest potential. Remember, although healing may seem challenging, it is worth the effort.

You might feel like you don't have the relationally mature mentors you need, and that's understandable. Let's pray right now that God brings someone into your life. He can do it!

# Check-In and Homework Time

# Part Two: Relational Circuits

By the end of unit two, you may be thinking, *How do I get my relational circuits back on?*

When you experience burnout, stress, tragedy, constant busyness, conflicts, and distractions, you may find that your relational circuits are turned off. To reconnect and grow with God as well as to be in tune with our loved ones, we will need to establish new habits that can help turn those circuits back on. Karl Lehman has written about these very habits in *The Immanuel Approach* and *Outsmarting Yourself*; when focus is given to teachings on attunement, calming exercises, practices of gratitude, and simple humor, then relational circuits can be turned back on and joy can be found!

Can you stop to consider how pillars of our faith created connections and healthy relationships? Consider how David spoke *of* and *to* God.

The following psalm of David was meant to be sung:

> "I will praise you, Lord, with all my heart;
>
> I will tell of all the marvelous things you have done" (Psalm 9:1).

# Mental Habits for Gratitude

Expressing gratitude to God and to others can uplift your spirits and, in turn, bring you joy and activate your circuits.

1. Do you actively practice gratitude?

2. What are some ways you can improve your practice of gratitude?

# Physical Habits to Help Bring Calming

Did you know physical exercise can turn on relational circuits? It may seem silly, but right yawn and left yawn, breathe and scrunch, how about a holler, box breathing, and knock to wake up the attachment center can all re-center us to a place to turn our relational circuits back on.

### Right Yawn and Left Yawn

Take a deep breath, turn to the right, and yawn. At the exhale, say a Bible verse, and repeat for the left side.

### Breathe and Scrunch

Act startled or upset, and then recite a Bible verse on the exhale.

### How about a Holler?

Sometimes, when the weight of the world gets too heavy to carry, hollering into a pillow can be a way to let it all out—raw, honest, and between you and God. God showed me this method when I was frustrated beyond belief one day. Life was throwing some serious situations beyond my control, one after another. In an attempt to distract myself while cleaning, I bumped my head on a cupboard. That's when I just let out such a holler, and I felt the Holy Spirit say, "Just let it all out!" So I did. Afterward, a calm came over me. God knew I needed to release all those emotions and give them to Him. Remember, it's not about losing

control; it's about releasing what's been building up inside before it hardens your heart. That cry, even if it's muffled, can be a kind of prayer—a physical way to lay your burdens down. In letting those emotions out, your nervous system gets a chance to settle, and your spirit can breathe again. Afterward, there's often a stillness, like God's quiet comfort meeting you in the space you made by letting go.

### Box Breathing[37]

Imagine running your finger up the side of a box while you breathe in for five seconds. Then imagine running your finger across the top of a box while holding your breath for five seconds. Slowly exhale for five seconds while picturing your finger running down the next side of the box. Finally, pause for five seconds while you imagine your finger traveling across the fourth side of the box. Repeat as needed!

### Knock to Wake Up the Attachment Center

Breathing and tapping combined is another helpful breathing exercise that you can use to turn on relational circuits and pull your mind away from stress. Breathe in deeply while tapping your chest at the same time. Breathe out and massage the same spot that you just tapped, and then recite a Scripture on the exhale. Repeat four times.

Look online or in my suggested resources for details on how to do these exercises or others.[38] Does doing those exercises sound silly?

Did you also know that doing things that seem silly can help to reset the brain? I know how helpful breath exercises can be from firsthand experience. So why not try them? This week, practice paying attention to when your circuits are on and off.

# Build Your Capacity for Joy

Joy may feel like one of those terms that is difficult to define, right? It is different from happiness. When you are aware of the role of relational circuits, you have the chance to build your capacity for joy through genuine connections when your relational circuits are turned on. Serotonin, as you may already know, is a neurotransmitter that's present in your brain and your intestines! It can act as a hormone would and affects your mood, digestion, and sleep. God has created us in amazingly complex and interesting ways! When someone expresses joy in their expressions and words during our conversations, it creates

---

37 Marcus Warner and Chris Coursey, *The 4 Habits of Joy-Filled People* (Northfield Publishing, 2023), 53.
38 Chris Coursey, *The Joy Switch* (Northfield Publishing, 2021), 135.

a serotonin reaction.[39] I often leave those interactions feeling uplifted and more joyful, as if our shared moments have added light to my spirit. Connecting with your herd, or the people in your community, has the power to act on you in much the same way as healthy levels of serotonin can, but your relational circuits need to be open and receptive!

Read the Bible verses below:

> "Be happy with those who are happy, and weep with those who weep. Live in harmony with each other. Don't be too proud to enjoy the company of ordinary people. And don't think you know it all!" (Romans 12:15–16).

> "Though good advice lies deep within the heart, a person with understanding will draw it out" (Proverbs 20:5).

1. How did those Bible verses speak to your heart?

2. After reading about relational circuits, do you think yours are mostly on or off?

3. Look back at pages 45–47 on relational circuits. Can you think of someone who is a healthy mentor who is also good at having their relational circuits turned on?

4. We are so blessed because God always has His relational circuits turned on. Reflect on that reality, and write out two things you are grateful for in connection with God's connection.

---

39    Warner and Coursey, *The 4 Habits of Joy-Filled People*, 37–38.

# Relationship Bonds

God has blessed His creation—both horses and people—with the gift of community. Yet that gift can sometimes require discernment and perseverance. Look at what the Bible says about relationships.

"Do not be unequally yoked with unbelievers. For what partnership has righteousness with lawlessness? Or what fellowship has light with darkness?" (2 Corinthians 6:14 ESV).

"Greater love has no one than this, that someone lay down his life for his friends" (John 15:13 ESV).

"Therefore encourage one another and build one another up, just as you are doing" (1 Thessalonians 5:11 ESV).

"With all humility and gentleness, with patience, bearing with one another in love. Eager to maintain the unity of the Spirit in the bond of peace" (Ephesians 4:2 ESV).

As you read through those verses, were you able to hear God's voice speaking to you? Hebrews 4:12 says that "the word of God is living and active" (ESV). What stood out to you from these four Scriptures?

Earlier in the workbook, when you read about relational circuits, you were also introduced to *sound attachments* and *lame attachments*. Being aware of sound attachments and lame attachments is so important. Who we are around rubs off on us. I came up with an acrostic illustration to help us decipher sound and lame attachments. These words and phrases are a guiding light for Our Healing Farm as we consider relationship bonds through our FBEAP sessions.

**S** STRONG, SINCERE, SOFT-SPOKEN, SELFLESS, SECURE, AND SUPPORTIVE

**O** OBSERVANT, OBEDIENT TO GOD, AND OPTIMISTIC

**U** UNDERSTANDING, UNCONDITIONAL, UPBEAT, USEFUL, UNIFIED, AND UNSELFISH

**N** NURTURING, NEIGHBORLY, NICE, NOBLE, AND NOTEWORTHY

**D** DEVOTED TO GOD, DEPENDABLE, DETERMINED, DELIGHTFUL, AND DECISIVE

**L** LIMITED, LIFE-SUCKING, LACKLUSTER, LOOSE-LIPPED, LOST, LUKEWARM, LAZY, AND LYING

**A** ABANDONING, ABRASIVE, ABUSIVE, ANNOYING, ARROGANT, AGGRESSIVE, ADDICTED, AND AVOIDANT

**M** MEDDLESOME, MANIPULATIVE, MALICIOUS, MISALIGNED, MANNERLESS, AND MERCILESS

**E** EMPTY, EDGY, ENVIOUS, ELUSIVE, ERRATIC, EXASPERATING, EGOTISTICAL, AND EXPLOITATIVE

As you take a look at these traits and behaviors, you might feel surprised or even convicted. Do you see some of your own behaviors or traits in these words? This isn't just a chance to look outward toward the people you spend your time with; it's also a great chance for you to reflect on and work toward a sound mindset instead of staying stuck in a lame one. This chance to meditate on the words associated with SOUND and LAME can also give you a clearer picture of the people in your lives and how they act. This will help you figure out which relationships are sound and will build you up through relational bonds.

## Check-In and Homework Time

## Part One: Relational Bonds

1.  Who in your life is a sound attachment?

2. Who in your life is a lame attachment?

3. Do you gravitate toward sound or lame attachments?

4. Are you a sound attachment or a lame attachment?

Sometimes living with our wounds can leave us with lame tendencies. However, remember that there is hope in God. We can transform and become everything God intends us to be with hard work. When Paul wrote to the people in Philippi, he said, "And I am certain that God, who began the good work within you, will continue his work until it is finally finished on the day when Christ Jesus returns" (Philippians 1:6). That promise is given to you and to me too! The Enemy, Satan, will seek to keep you in this state of limitation through lame attachments because he wants to lead God's people to darkness (oppression) and death.

But that does not have to be your path!

Remember to build up your people who are sound attachments by showing gratitude—it is joy-building! If you are left feeling like you are more of a lame attachment, give God thanks for revealing that to you so you can change. As you begin to heal, you will become more sound in your relational attachments; what a blessing that our God can change us!

If you feel you are a sound attachment for others, are you doing everything you can to come alongside them to help them connect relationally with you and God? Remember, this can create joy for both you and the person you are mentoring. We need mentors! Are your relational circuits on to help others?

Part of being a sound attachment is the ability to encourage people in a positive way. In the horse world, spurs often get a bad reputation because some people view them as inhumane. However, like many things, spurs can be used in a healthy manner or abused, depending on how they are applied. If you harshly ask a horse to respond, leaving marks or even scars, then you are hurting the animal. On the other hand, if you use a spur as a gentle cue to guide the horse into movements, it becomes an extension of your foot.

We have a horse on our farm named Elwood who is completely spur-trained. Our trainer always emphasizes a holistic and caring approach, so spurs are meant to guide, not inflict pain. Using a bit in a horse's mouth while constantly pulling can be painful as well. This is why leg training can be so much better. Trust me; a horse prefers a gentle push from your leg or spur over being yanked on its mouth! I've seen it time and time again.

However, just as spurs can be used positively in training, they can have a negative effect if misused by someone without proper training. When we encourage our loved ones, it's essential to consider how we are doing it. Are we building them up, or are we pushing them in the wrong direction? Our words have the power to bring happiness or pain to others. If we fail to recognize the positive qualities in our loved ones, they may not see the value we have for them. If you notice something positive, encourage that person through acknowledging what he or she has done! Give them the recognition they deserve. When we uplift others, it not only helps the person we are encouraging, but it also pleases God, which in turn fulfills our souls.

Has any of this talk of spurs and bridles shown you that you don't have anyone guiding you through your life? There are times in everyone's life when guidance from a sound attachment is critical. Are you struggling and need a sound attachment for a mentor? Please pay attention to your relational circuits. Are they on? Do you want help finding a relational connection? Sometimes we become so stuck that we just want to isolate. If this is where

you are right now, remember that God wants you to live a herd-like life that is relational with others. As you heal, be open to having sound attachments and relational connections.

Look up the Bible verses I have chosen for you and reflect on how they relate to relational bonds below:

Ephesians 4:29          1 Thessalonians 5:14          Philippians 2:4

These verses point us to spurring people on in positive ways. If you aren't familiar with spurs or even have a negative connotation of them, then think back to how I explained the difference between the proper and improper use of them. One of the best ways to improve relationships is to spur each other on!

1. Do you think you are good at spurring people on?

2. Do you feel spurred on by anyone?

If you answered no to either of those questions, I can imagine that it weighs heavily on your heart. I know it does on mine too. No one should have to go through life without feeling like someone is cheering for them. This is why it's so important to encourage others when we feel inspired to do so! That's how strong herds are built!

## Check-In and Homework Time

## Part Two: What You Hang Your Hat On and Giving the Enemy the Boot

As we have already discussed, it's so important that we have sound attachments that spur us on in positivity. Now, let's talk about what you hang your hat on or who you hang it with. Allowing strongholds or lame people run by their own strongholds into your life can affect your ability to heal—or even your desire to heal!

1. Are there any lame people you know who are held down by strongholds and are keeping you from achieving healing?

2. Do you believe in spiritual warfare? Have you ever prayed against it in your life?

"Therefore put on the full armor of God, so that when the day of evil comes, you may be able to stand your ground, and after you have done everything, to stand" (Ephesians 6:13 NIV).

In the verse above, do you see how it says "when" and not "if the day of evil comes"? Friend, it's not *if* we will battle; it's *when*!

Look up Ephesians 6:14–17; then define each part of the armor of God below:

    Belt of truth -

    Breastplate of righteousness -

    Shoes of the gospel of peace -

    Shield of faith -

    Helmet of salvation -

    Sword of the Spirit -

As you can see, God has given us tools to fight with. There is a whole armory sent for us to wear in battle.

Spiritual warfare can seem scary, but I assure you, God is so much more powerful than any stronghold against you or me.

"Then the seventy-two returned with joy, saying, 'Lord, even the demons are subject to us in your name!' And He said to them, 'I saw Satan fall like lightning from heaven. Behold, I give you the authority to trample on serpents and scorpions, and over all the power of the enemy, and nothing shall by any means hurt you" (Luke 10:17–19 NKJV).

As you can see in the verse above, you have the authority to pray against the warfare against or even upon you!

3. Do you have any strongholds you need to pray against today?

4. Is anything stopping you from giving the Enemy the boot?

If spiritual warfare is new to you, as it was for me over a decade ago, I encourage you to explore it further. Gaining knowledge and awareness about spiritual warfare can help ensure it doesn't become a roadblock on your healing journey.

Part of herd life is ensuring we hang our hats on God's principles and not alone, but instead with sound relationships who will come alongside you and help give the Enemy the boot!

## Checking In on FBEAP – Foundational Principle: Relationship Zones

1. When it comes to Relationship Zones, do you tend to get ahead of God?

2. Does God guide your life, or do you?

Friend, part of healing is releasing control to God and not getting ahead of Him. Letting the Holy Spirit guide and energize us is essential to receive healing.

I truly hope that after completing the second week of this study, you have developed a deeper appreciation for the incredible gift that the Holy Spirit is in our lives, as well as the immense need for a life surrounded by a healthy herd. In the next unit, we will be exploring joy, one of my favorite topics!

# Prayers and Praises

*It's time for*

# Unit 3

## Say Howdy and Spark Some Joy!

## Unit 3

# Say Howdy and Spark Some Joy!

This week, I am excited to share the third most important lesson I've learned on my healing journey. While living a life led by the Holy Spirit is my top priority, understanding the concept of sparking joy is nearly as crucial. Some may dismiss this idea as trivial, but I can wholeheartedly assure you that embracing joy has profoundly transformed my life, and for that, I am immensely grateful to God.

### Here's some quick brain science behind joy:

Dr. Allan Schore was the first to discover how powerful joy is for the brain. He found that our brain functions best when it is experiencing joy.[40]

Our brains consist of two halves, or hemispheres: the left and the right. The right half is our main control hub, which many call the "joy center." This hemisphere is associated with seven distinct emotions:[41]

1. Joy
2. Fear
3. Sadness
4. Disgust
5. Hopelessness
6. Anger
7. Shame

The Lord bestowed upon us seven emotions. Joy is the emotion that enables us to live our healthiest lives and flourish. Additionally, six emotions act as our protectors. All these emotions are essential in safeguarding us from enduring pain. As *Living From the Heart Jesus Gave You* explains, when our joy strength and joy center are developed enough, we can regulate our challenging emotions and find our way back to joy.[42]

---

40  Warner and Coursey, *The 4 Habits of Joy-Filled People*, 31–32.
41  Warner and Coursey, *The 4 Habits of Joy-Filled People*, 128.
42  Friesen, *Living From the Heart Jesus Gave You*, 28.

# ★ ★ ★
# The Protecting Emotions

The following emotions can be studied on truly deep levels in Warner and Coursey's book,[43] but let's briefly explore each one here:

**Anger -** This intense emotion arises when you want something unfair or distressing to stop. It's completely normal to experience feelings of anger, but it's crucial that you find your way back to joy.

**Shame -** This emotion stems from a lack of joy and feelings of not being seen, heard, or appreciated. It brings about a sense of guilt regarding yourself and your actions. When shame becomes toxic, especially if it's inflicted regularly by others, it can trap you.

**Disgust -** This feeling manifests when you are repulsed and may even evoke nausea. People often feel this when confronted with someone exhibiting incompetence. Additionally, having low self-esteem can lead to a sense of disgust about how you perceive yourself.

**Sadness -** This emotion emerges from the profound acknowledgment of a loss that once brought you true joy. Grief is part of this experience.

**Fear -** When your brain detects possible dangers, it initiates a physical response. During these times, it is possible to summon courage despite your fears. Anxiety and worry are also part of this emotion and arise from your doubts about the future and what may come.

**Hopeless -** This emotion is linked to feelings of despair. It occurs when individuals feel a lack of control and see the possibility of resolving their issues as unattainable.

---

43    Warner and Coursey, *The 4 Habits of Joy-Filled People*, 128–40.

# The Left Brain vs. The Right Brain

In my search for joy—this unit's focus—I have come across some great resources to dive deeper into the study of emotions and how they develop in the brain. Hendricks and Wilder have shared their own research on the capabilities of each hemisphere of the brain, and I will share the bare bones of that below.[44] If you want to learn more, please get a copy of *The Other Half of Church.*

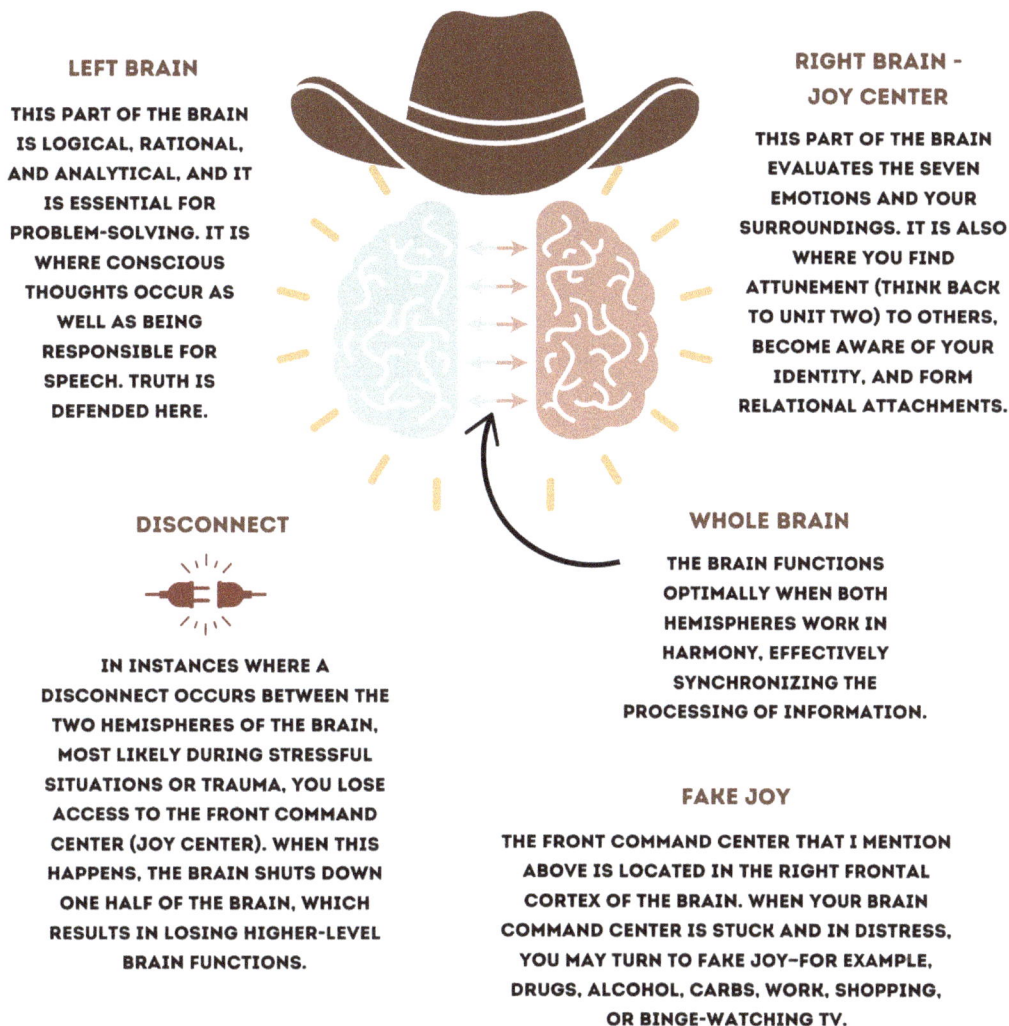

**LEFT BRAIN**

THIS PART OF THE BRAIN IS LOGICAL, RATIONAL, AND ANALYTICAL, AND IT IS ESSENTIAL FOR PROBLEM-SOLVING. IT IS WHERE CONSCIOUS THOUGHTS OCCUR AS WELL AS BEING RESPONSIBLE FOR SPEECH. TRUTH IS DEFENDED HERE.

**RIGHT BRAIN - JOY CENTER**

THIS PART OF THE BRAIN EVALUATES THE SEVEN EMOTIONS AND YOUR SURROUNDINGS. IT IS ALSO WHERE YOU FIND ATTUNEMENT (THINK BACK TO UNIT TWO) TO OTHERS, BECOME AWARE OF YOUR IDENTITY, AND FORM RELATIONAL ATTACHMENTS.

**DISCONNECT**

IN INSTANCES WHERE A DISCONNECT OCCURS BETWEEN THE TWO HEMISPHERES OF THE BRAIN, MOST LIKELY DURING STRESSFUL SITUATIONS OR TRAUMA, YOU LOSE ACCESS TO THE FRONT COMMAND CENTER (JOY CENTER). WHEN THIS HAPPENS, THE BRAIN SHUTS DOWN ONE HALF OF THE BRAIN, WHICH RESULTS IN LOSING HIGHER-LEVEL BRAIN FUNCTIONS.

**WHOLE BRAIN**

THE BRAIN FUNCTIONS OPTIMALLY WHEN BOTH HEMISPHERES WORK IN HARMONY, EFFECTIVELY SYNCHRONIZING THE PROCESSING OF INFORMATION.

**FAKE JOY**

THE FRONT COMMAND CENTER THAT I MENTION ABOVE IS LOCATED IN THE RIGHT FRONTAL CORTEX OF THE BRAIN. WHEN YOUR BRAIN COMMAND CENTER IS STUCK AND IN DISTRESS, YOU MAY TURN TO FAKE JOY—FOR EXAMPLE, DRUGS, ALCOHOL, CARBS, WORK, SHOPPING, OR BINGE-WATCHING TV.

45 46 47 48

Did you notice that the explanation for the right brain includes the phrase "joy center"? Let's get even more specific at pinpointing where joy can be found in this amazing organ.

---

44    Michel Hendricks and Jim Wilder, *The Other Half of Church* (Moody Publishers, 2020), 18–28.
45    Hendricks and Wilder, *The Other Half of Church*, 26–27.
46    Warner and Coursey, *The 4 Habits of Joy-Filled People*, 43.
47    Warner and Coursey, *The 4 Habits of Joy-Filled People*, 39–44.
48    E. James Wilder et al., *Joy Starts Here* (Life Model Works™, 2021), 39, 44–47.

## Right Pre-Frontal Cortex: The Joy Center

**RIGHT PRE-FRONTAL CORTEX** →

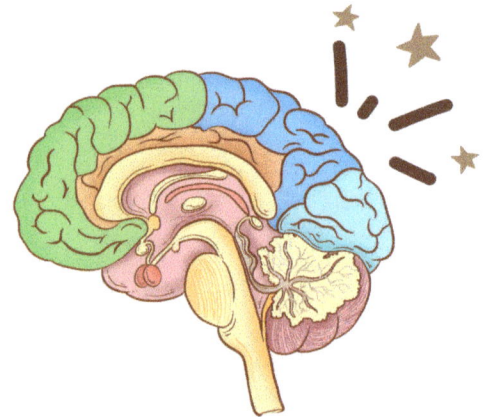

The truly remarkable aspect of the joy center is its capacity for growth, meaning it's never too late to heal. The joy center is situated in the right orbital area of the prefrontal cortex, which is responsible for our highest functions of the brain. While it is mostly immature at birth, it evolves into an emotional command center as we grow. Experiencing relational joy contributes to the ongoing development of the joy center. However, if the joy center stays underdeveloped, it may become limited in size, making it difficult to feel relational joy under stress. This lack of development can also result in challenges when trying to express our true selves during times of distress.[49]

Understanding the science of the brain and embracing God's design for how we function is vital to living the abundant life He has called us to.

## Let's Take a Joy Ride!

I created a helpful illustration on the next page to better understand the phrase "joy ride," but let me explain it to you now in words.

What brings safety and joy to a horse? Being at peace with its herd in a safe place can lead to joy for a horse. Have you ever been on a trail ride and had the horse you were riding suddenly turn around and race back to the barn? That happened to my poor mother while we were on vacation years ago. Do you think her horse wanted to be naughty? Or did it simply want to be at its favorite place that brings peace, joy, and stability? The horse knows it will be taken care of there. That's why it was fitting to represent the barn as the joy center in my illustration. Remember, when we are in a state of joy, we function at our best.

---

49    Warner and Coursey, *The 4 Habits of Joy-Filled People*, 39.

Next, you will see horses carrying our emotions down a trail away from the barn (our joy). Those horses want nothing more than to leave our emotions and take us back to the barn, but they are stuck until we give them permission.

You need to allow yourself to acknowledge feelings but also let go of them. Part of that process requires addressing that you have past wounds that need healing. If you head down a trail with limited resources and get stuck, will you have enough to survive? No, you will run out of supplies. When you become trapped by difficult emotions, you'll start to lose the essential things that are needed to survive and thrive in life. Your body becomes exhausted and may even experience illness or feel like it's nearing the end of all strength.

It is critical that we take the trail back to joy.

Stick with me on this metaphor I'm presenting to you! I want you to think of that horse carrying you and your emotions. Would you let it get sick and possibly die? Of course not. So why would you allow yourself to remain stuck in difficult emotions? The answer *can* be the Enemy, but it is often unresolved emotions and trauma that keep you there unwillingly.

You are reading this because you are searching for something. You may just want to learn more about FBEAP, but I would guess that you are also looking for ways to heal, and FBEAP is just one way to get there! Part of the journey to hope and healing is through joy—that's why I have created a whole unit focused on it. It's crucial to begin filling your joy center so you can gradually find your way back to the barn. Remember, the barn is symbolic of your safe place, where you know you will be cared for and feel joy; it is where you can receive the things that give you life. By building your joy capacity, you give yourself the strength to return to the barn more easily when difficult moments come your way.[50]

Friend, please hear me say this next sentence loud and clear! Riding the trail back to joy and finding the strength to return to joyfulness does not imply that you don't feel heartache. Instead, it signifies that even during life's toughest challenges, you can find comfort in knowing that Jesus rides with us from the six trails of protecting emotions back to joy. Joy that is relational brings gladness to our hearts, even when the journey feels heavy.[51]

50     Friesen, *Living From the Heart Jesus Gave You*, 74–81.
51     Wilder and Hendricks, *The Other Half of Church*, 59.

HUMILIATION

**SHAME**

STUCK
DISTRESS

**HOPELESS**

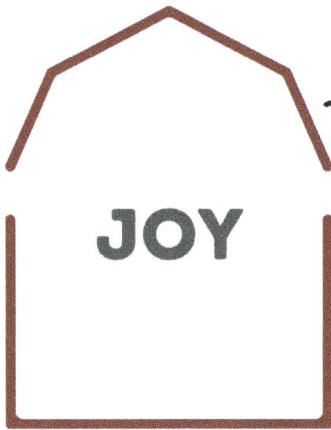

**JOY**

REPULSED

**DISGUST**

DEPRESSION
GRIEF

**SADNESS**

ANXIETY
WORRY
PANIC

**FEAR**

RAGE
BITTER
RESENTMENT

**ANGER**

# Growing Your Joy Center

As I mentioned back in the introduction, my journey to healing and hope has been a long process that was possible because of the knowledge I gained from two amazing organizations *and* from the information I gleaned from several excellent books. This section on relational joy centers is a prime example of that gathering of knowledge; my hope is that I can share what I have learned in a meaningful way! The concept of growing your joy center that you'll be reading about now is adapted from teachings found in *The Immanuel Approach for Emotional Healing for Life*,[52] *The 4 Habits of Joy-Filled People*,[53] and *The Other Half of Church*.[54] Each of these books on its own is amazing, but for our purposes at Our Healing Farm and this workbook, I've created several aspects to focus on.

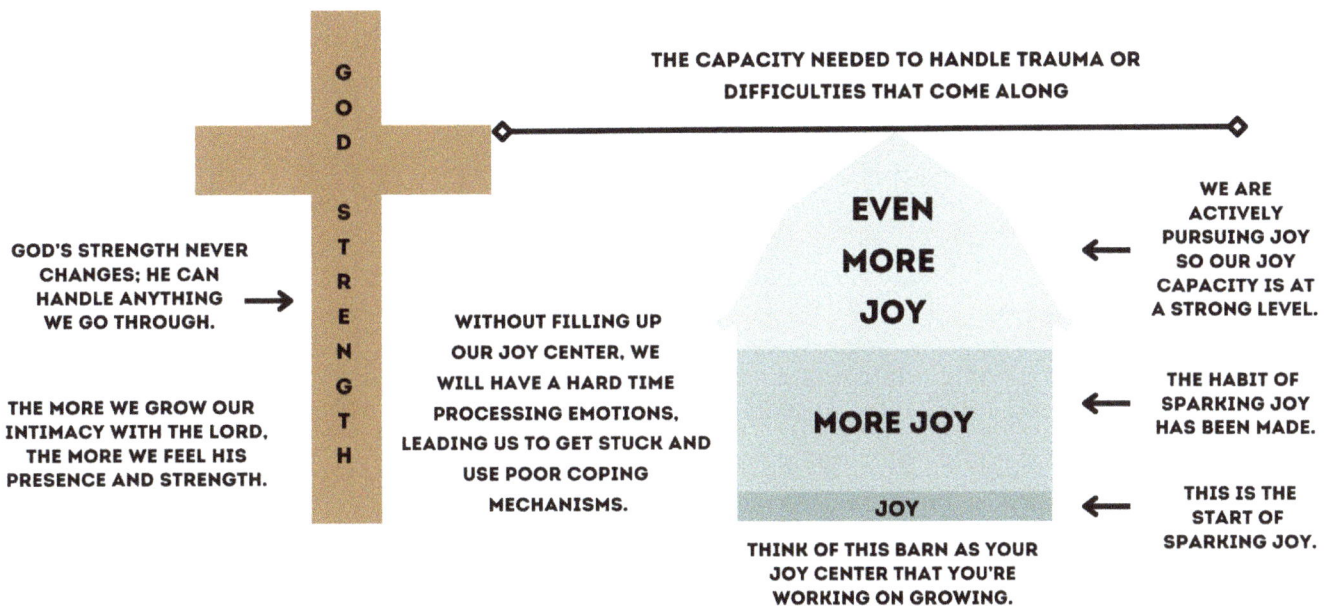

THE CAPACITY NEEDED TO HANDLE TRAUMA OR DIFFICULTIES THAT COME ALONG

GOD STRENGTH

GOD'S STRENGTH NEVER CHANGES; HE CAN HANDLE ANYTHING WE GO THROUGH.

THE MORE WE GROW OUR INTIMACY WITH THE LORD, THE MORE WE FEEL HIS PRESENCE AND STRENGTH.

WITHOUT FILLING UP OUR JOY CENTER, WE WILL HAVE A HARD TIME PROCESSING EMOTIONS, LEADING US TO GET STUCK AND USE POOR COPING MECHANISMS.

EVEN MORE JOY

MORE JOY

JOY

WE ARE ACTIVELY PURSUING JOY SO OUR JOY CAPACITY IS AT A STRONG LEVEL.

THE HABIT OF SPARKING JOY HAS BEEN MADE.

THIS IS THE START OF SPARKING JOY.

THINK OF THIS BARN AS YOUR JOY CENTER THAT YOU'RE WORKING ON GROWING.

---

52    Lehman, *The Immanuel Approach*, 73–83
53    Warner and Coursey, *The 4 Habits of Joy-Filled People*, 20–22.
54    Wilder and Hendricks, *The Other Half of Church*, 62–64.

## Ways to Fill Up Your Joy Center:

- Showing genuine concern and care for others
- Connecting with loved ones and listening to the Holy Spirit
- Enjoying playful moments together
- Welcoming loved ones with authenticity
- Practicing calmness and expressing gratitude
- MOST importantly, nurturing your relationship with the Lord

These are just six suggestions from *Living From the Heart Jesus Gave You*.[55] Refilling your joy center opens a route to confront the tougher emotions. When you are dealing with unresolved trauma and limited joy capacity, your brain might find it difficult to manage the emotions and memories that come up. It may distance itself (resulting in amnesia or dissociation) until your joy center and joy strength are robust enough to confront the trauma or unpleasant memories.[56] That is why it is essential to work alongside a trained professional to work through *severe* trauma. Sometimes that will require a licensed professional therapist. Remember, the FBEAP certified group at Our Healing Farm is not made up of professional therapists, but we *are* here to work alongside you in your journey to hope and healing.

In the book *Living From the Heart Jesus Gave You*, relational joy is described as "knowing who we are meant to be, as we see ourselves and others through the awareness and discernment of the heart that Jesus gives us."[57] Look back up to the list above. Out of the six points listed above, which do you find yourself practicing on a daily basis? This journey to healing may show you what you're already doing well, or it may be calling you to create new rhythms and routines.

Joy signifies that someone, especially God, is glad to be with me.[58] Joy becomes relational when we understand that God delights in our presence and that we experience joy when we're around someone who genuinely enjoys being with us. This feeling of joy arises from the sense of being valued by that person. Relational joy flourishes in meaningful connections with both God and others.

---

55    Friesen, *Living From the Heart Jesus Gave You*, 25.
56    Friesen, *Living From the Heart Jesus Gave You*, 76
57    Friesen, *Living From the Heart Jesus Gave You*, xii, 25–28.
58    This illustration was inspired by Friesen, *Living From the Heart Jesus Gave You*, 27.

# It's time for some

# Unit 3

# Check-Ins

## Check-In and Homework Time

## Relational Joy vs. Fake Joy

It's essential to distinguish between fake joy and relational joy. Relational joy is genuine joy and will fill your joy center capacity. When filling your joy center, think of relational joy like a water spigot turned on at full strength. In contrast, fake joy can be likened to a faucet that is shut off. It consists of non-relational experiences and often takes the form of addictions. These may include stimulants that activate the pleasure center in the brain and release dopamine, but unfortunately, they only provide a temporary fix. While they may offer a fleeting sense of happiness, that feeling soon wears off and leaves you craving more.

### Here are some examples of fake joy:[59]

- Foods that provide comfort, such as sugary items and carbohydrates
- Addictions related to work and performance
- Participating in activities primarily to gain approval from others
- Compulsions related to sex and pornography
- An ongoing desire for thrill and stimulation
- Binge-watching TV shows or obsessively consuming sports and other entertainment (includes cell phone dependencies)
- Using drugs and alcohol to numb emotional pain
- Compulsive gambling behaviors
- Developing codependent dynamics in relationships

A good rule of thumb to determine if joy is relational is to ask yourself if Jesus or someone you care about is glad to be with you in that moment. Additionally, expressing gratitude to God or the person involved in the moment is essential.

Friend, do you remember back in the beginning of this workbook when I told you I would be vulnerable through sharing my own story? Well, here is another unguarded moment. During my healing journey, I realized just how much I relied on fake joys to cope with my difficult emotions. I frequently found myself scrolling through my phone for hours and binge-watching TV series as my main sources of distraction. In unit five, titled "Say Howdy to Healthy Coping!," we will explore more effective coping skills.

---

59    Wilder, *Joy Starts Here*, 39–48.

1. Can you relate to any of the fake joys listed? Describe your feelings below:

2. When do you notice you turn to fake joy most?

Look up the Scriptures below and reflect:

**1 Corinthians 10:13**         **Galatians 5:19–21**         **Romans 13:14**

Can you see that fake joy is really a temptation of our flesh and is still the work of the Enemy? You may follow through with the fleshly temptation, and it may seem like a quick, gratifying fix, but it isn't authentic, lasting relational joy. In the long run, it doesn't make us feel better but instead just leaves us craving more.

## True Relational Joy

Does the idea of sparking all this relational joy seem overwhelming? Or perhaps you feel unsure about how to do it. That is understandable; I felt that way at first as well. However, remember that your joy center can continue to grow throughout your life, so you have plenty of time—your whole life—to learn and change.

Today we will focus on the little things that help us to spark joy!

"Always be joyful. Never stop praying. Be thankful in all circumstances, for this is God's will for you who belong to Christ Jesus" (1 Thessalonians 5:16–18).

When Paul, Silas, and Timothy wrote to the church in Thessalonica, they knew the people needed reminders to seek joy and perhaps could find it through continual prayer. Sometimes it's the little snippets of joy that you have to find in difficult situations that help fill your capacity. You may be able to find joy through prayer too, but here are some pathways to those prayers that you may not have considered.

## Little things that can spark joy:

- Stroll with someone special or walk while connecting with God (through prayer or by listening to worship music).

- Savor your favorite beverage while expressing thanks to God.

- Relish a beloved meal alongside a cherished person.

- Spend time outdoors in nature to connect with a loved one or with God.

- Share moments of laughter with someone dear.

- Share a joke with a loved one.

- Find joy in decorating your home and appreciate the happiness it will bring to others (you can express gratitude to God during the process).

- Enjoy cozy moments with a pet (pets are always happy to be with you).

- Light a candle and thank God for something He has done for you.

- Enjoy a bath and find stillness with the Lord.

- Reach out to a friend.

- Engage in a hobby with family members or infuse your activity with a sense of connection to God.

- Keep an ongoing journal with the sense of gratitude you feel upon returning home after a long day.

- Tidy up (if it brings you joy).

- Spend time outdoors gardening while fostering a connection with God or a loved one.

- Prepare a favorite dish alongside a loved one.

- Receive a warm hug from someone dear to you.

- Reflect on a moment when someone has shared something meaningful with you.

There are *countless* other experiences that could be added to this already lengthy list, but as long as you connect with a loved one or God, you can spark *true joy*! Perhaps the most important thing I can share is to pay attention to when you are feeling joy. It can be as small as a tiny feeling. Then I want you to say to yourself that you just felt joy. When you say it, you are forming a new habit of acknowledging joy, which benefits your joy center. Additionally, it's essential that you take time to thank the Lord for this joyful experience, which brings gratitude in and makes it a relational experience as well. You connect with God when you express gratitude, worship Him, spend time being still in the Holy Spirit's presence, and engage in prayer.

Do you struggle to experience joy? If you find yourself feeling this way, it's a normal reaction that suggests you may need healing. Try to notice even the smallest moments of joy; they are present around you. It's important to learn how to seek out these opportunities or to actively search for moments that bring you joy.

1. Reflect on joyful moments you've experienced lately. Write out one or two of them here.

2. When you think about them, how do you feel in your mind and body?

3. Do you think that Jesus sparked joy while He was here on earth?

Look up these Bible verses and reflect on each one:

**John 15:11**                      **Matthew 18:13**                 **Matthew 5:12**

After reflecting on those verses, do you think Jesus liked to spark joy? I find it hard to believe that Jesus walked around with a serious demeanor, like a stick in the mud. Who would want to follow Him if He didn't exude joy at least part of the time? His disciples left their homes, families, and trades to follow Him—can you imagine doing that for a man who was miserable? I am sure that you have a clear understanding of the three verses I've pulled out to highlight this concept, but I'll share some quick insights as well. John 15:11 mentions being filled with joy to overflowing. I believe Jesus truly understands the vital importance of joy. In Matthew 18:13, Jesus speaks of the joy of finding the lost. I believe He cherishes people, and joy is what flows from receiving them into His flock. Matthew 5:12 encourages us to find joy even during times of persecution. Additionally, I think Jesus was deeply connected to those around Him. He achieved this by engaging relationally, which allowed Him to share joy with others.

The last verse noted above might be the most difficult or challenging of the three I've chosen to have you meditate on. This doesn't imply we need to mask our struggles with fake joy; rather, it calls us to rise above negativity. How can God use us to our fullest potential if we remain stuck?

# Time to Take Another Joy Ride!

Take a moment to sit quietly with the Holy Spirit and ask Him to help you identify any emotions that you might be feeling stuck with. Once you have recognized these emotions, draw a line or trail from joy to the specific emotion. Understanding the emotions we are stuck in is crucial for our healing. Spend some time in prayer with the Lord, and search for a Scripture that can help you combat those feelings.

HUMILIATION

SHAME

STUCK
DISTRESS

HOPELESS

REPULSED

DISGUST

DEPRESSION
GRIEF

SADNESS

ANXIETY
WORRY
PANIC

FEAR

RAGE
BITTER
RESENTMENT

ANGER

JOY

# Access Your Joy Center and Relationship with Your Lord

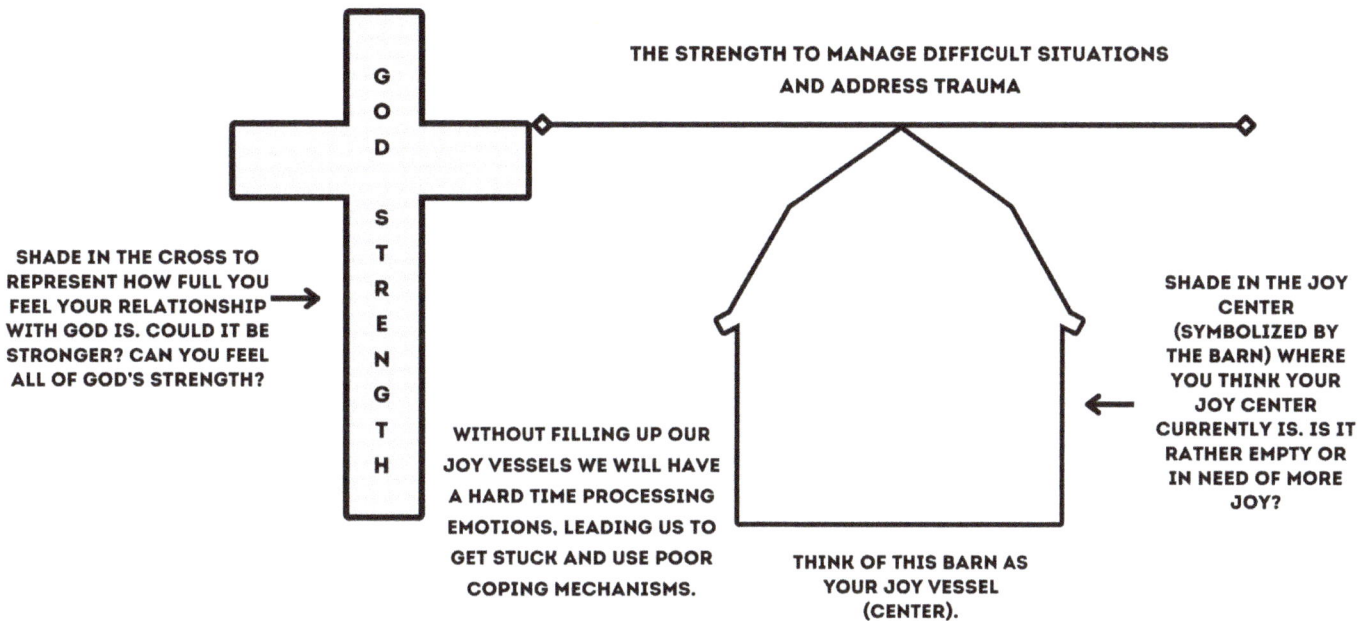

**THE STRENGTH TO MANAGE DIFFICULT SITUATIONS AND ADDRESS TRAUMA**

**G O D   S T R E N G T H**

SHADE IN THE CROSS TO REPRESENT HOW FULL YOU FEEL YOUR RELATIONSHIP WITH GOD IS. COULD IT BE STRONGER? CAN YOU FEEL ALL OF GOD'S STRENGTH?

WITHOUT FILLING UP OUR JOY VESSELS WE WILL HAVE A HARD TIME PROCESSING EMOTIONS, LEADING US TO GET STUCK AND USE POOR COPING MECHANISMS.

THINK OF THIS BARN AS YOUR JOY VESSEL (CENTER).

SHADE IN THE JOY CENTER (SYMBOLIZED BY THE BARN) WHERE YOU THINK YOUR JOY CENTER CURRENTLY IS. IS IT RATHER EMPTY OR IN NEED OF MORE JOY?

1. Shade in the cross to represent how full you feel your relationship with God is. Could it be stronger? Can you feel all of God's strength?

2. Shade in the joy center (symbolized by the barn) where you think your joy center currently is. Is it rather empty or in need of *more* joy?

In the exercise above, it's important to *honestly* assess your current relationship with the Lord and how full you feel your joy center is. This assessment helps us understand your capacity to handle difficult times. God's strength is never-ending, and you will feel it most when you strive for a closer walk with Him.

3. Take a moment to shade in the cross above to represent your current relationship with God. Is it full, reflecting time spent together, or is it emptier because God wants more from you?

4. Next, evaluate how full you think your joy center is. Is it operating at full capacity, is it at mid-level, or is it nearly empty?

Remember, with time you can grow both your joy and your relationship with God, which equips you with the strength to face all the challenges life throws your way. Isn't that wonderful? Don't feel discouraged if you barely shaded in the cross and barn; recognizing areas that need improvement can be the first step into a healing experience.

Developing new habits, which you will learn about in this book, can help get you back on track. So don't lose hope! On the next few pages, we introduce creating joy moments so we can get back to joy and fill our joy vessels!

## Creating Joyful Moments

An important step on your healing journey is to create moments of joy that you can revisit, especially during the tougher times. It's completely normal for emotions to surface unexpectedly; this may leave you feeling stuck or overwhelmed. In those moments, having a joyful moment to turn to and remember can be incredibly grounding and comforting. As Wilder teaches, a great way to find joy is remembering times we felt relationally connected to God or another person and then following the memory with a time of gratitude with the Lord.[60]

Today I invite you to sit quietly with the Holy Spirit and ask for guidance in recalling a time when you experienced a sense of relational joy that evokes gratitude. When you're ready, take a moment to write it down on the next page after my breakdown of YEEHAW! If you find yourself saying, "I can't remember a joyful moment because of my past," that's perfectly understandable. Trauma can often cloud our memories. However, remember that we all find beauty in the things around us. Maybe it's your favorite beach, a park you like to walk in, or God's beautiful handiwork of trees changing colors in the fall. We all have something for which we can be grateful. Ask God to help you remember something.

---

60    Wilder and Hendricks, *The Other Half of Church*, 218–19.

★ ★ ★

**Y** YOU CAN FIND JOY.
TELL YOURSELF THAT!

**E** ENGAGE WITH THE HOLY SPIRIT.
BE STILL AND LISTEN.

**E** ENCOURAGE YOURSELF TO RECALL A JOYFUL
MOMENT OF GRATITUDE FROM YOUR MEMORY.

**H** HOLD ONTO THAT MOMENT AS LONG
AS YOU CAN, UP TO FIVE MINUTES.

**A** ASSESS HOW YOU FEEL IN YOUR
MIND AND BODY.

**W** WELCOME THE FEELING OF JOY
AND GIVE THE LORD GRATITUDE.

Try to repeat this one to three times a day.

1. Write your joy moment:

Hold onto that moment for as long as you can. Can you do it for up to five minutes?

2. Assess how you feel in your mind and body; then write out notes:

Welcome the feeling of joy and give the Lord gratitude. Try to repeat this exercise every day, even multiple times![61]

---

61     This exercise was adapted from Wilder and Hendricks, *The Other Half of Church*, 217–20.

★ ★ ★

# Prayers and Praises

# It's time for
## Unit 4
## Howdy! Are You Stuck?

# Howdy! Are You Stuck?

Now that we've discussed the importance of joy, let's explore trauma. Remember, joy helps you navigate life's challenges. That isn't just an anecdotal sentiment—it's a biblical truth that you meditated on earlier in this study! While transitioning from *joy* to *trauma* may seem like an awkward move, it is actually a conscious choice that I have made as I try to lead you through this path.

Sadly, trauma is a reality in this fallen world that does not discriminate; men and women of all ages, ethnicities, and socioeconomic statuses must endure it. Many older generations lacked an understanding of trauma and its effects as the science was not developed at the time. Today we can recognize trauma's impact on the brain, and that enables us to address and heal from it. I've learned to forgive my childhood experiences, knowing that my parents and their generation didn't understand either.

After years of parenting without this knowledge, I've apologized to my children for my mistakes; that act of apologizing has been healing. This teaches them that while everyone makes mistakes, it's essential to apologize and strive for improvement.

You may or may not have firsthand experiences with trauma. However, even if **you** don't have personal experience with trauma, I am sure you know someone who does. I once spoke to a woman who dismissed trauma as just "normal life." Ironically, she was struggling with significant challenges in her own family. I hope she will one day recognize the need for healing. Friend, choosing to address your trauma is about surrendering to God's process and letting go of control. I see broken families in chaos everywhere, but it doesn't have to be this way. While we can't change the past, we can heal and create a better future for the next generation. Isn't that powerful?

# Trauma A

Embarking on the journey of healing from trauma can be challenging, and it's important to start by recognizing and acknowledging the wounds you carry within. According to the research presented in *Living From the Heart Jesus Gave You,* trauma can generally be broken down into two main categories.[62]

Trauma A occurs when individuals lack those nurturing and positive experiences that are essential for their emotional well-being. When people don't receive these vital elements, it can lead to significant struggles in relationships with others. If you are working through healing from trauma, then it's completely understandable for painful emotions to surface as you confront the absence of what you deserved. According to Friesen's book, traumas that fit into this first category can leave you feeling like there's a deep fracture in your soul.[63]

Many people find it hard to fully acknowledge the impact of Trauma A, often out of fear or a desire to avoid their pain. This denial can cause feelings of being lost, unworthy, and hesitant to trust yourself or those around you, which can ultimately wear away at your confidence and sense of identity. It's important to recognize that these feelings are valid and that you are not alone in this experience.

## Examples of Trauma A:

- Feeling unappreciated or undervalued by those who matter most to you
- Having parents who failed to acknowledge and celebrate the strengths of your identity
- Experiencing a shortage of joy from those you care about
- Lacking sufficient affection and warmth in your relationships
- Facing challenges with inadequate food, housing, clothing, and access to medical and dental care
- Not having well-defined boundaries or guidelines to follow

- Missing opportunities to explore and nurture your personal talents and abilities
- Not being taught how to confront difficult challenges and persist until you achieve competence
- Not experiencing significant amounts of non-sexual physical affection, which can mean missing out on opportunities to sit on laps, to be embraced, and to have the ability to disengage when you feel you've had enough

---

62    Friesen, *Living From the Heart Jesus Gave You*, 82–95.
63    Friesen, *Living From the Heart Jesus Gave You*, 84.

# Trauma B

Trauma B often arises from painful experiences that can deeply affect one's mind, and this can lead to what feels like what Friesen calls "fractures of the mind."[64] When individuals struggle with unresolved emotions from these experiences, it can be incredibly challenging to find a way back to joy. It's important to recognize that sometimes the mind will try to protect itself through amnesia related to traumatic events; this causes the individual to forget the pain. Unfortunately, this can create a sense of disconnection from one's own memories.[65] However, when both our bodies and the Holy Spirit are aligned, there is hope of recovering those lost memories. Embracing this healing journey is vital as unaddressed memories can linger and weigh people down. Confronting the past can be a crucial step toward healing and finding peace as a way to move forward.

## Examples of Trauma B:

- Physical abuse
- Sexual misconduct, such as inappropriate touching, exposure to pornography, or an adult sharing sexual content
- Severe spanking that leaves bruises (marks) and emotional wounds
- Neglect or abandonment
- Verbal mistreatment or derogatory name-calling
- Torture or abuse associated with satanic rituals
- Observing someone being harmed
- Emotional or psychological mistreatment
- Exposure to cults
- Bullying
- Traumatic grief

- Accidents
- Terrorism, mass violence, and mass shootings
- Fighting in war
- Life-threatening illnesses
- Refugee trauma
- Natural disaster trauma
- Community violence
- Disaster trauma (such as a house fire)
- Medical trauma (including childbirth, doctor negligence, physical injuries, etc.)
- Sex trafficking
- Infidelity
- Financial trauma
- Secondhand trauma (witnessing tragic events, such as the loss of a life)

---

64    Friesen, *Living From the Heart Jesus Gave You*, 87.
65    Friesen, *Living From the Heart Jesus Gave You*, 87.

Friend, I know that the topic of trauma is a difficult one. Since you are working through this study from Our Healing Farm, I know there is a high likelihood that you yourself are searching for healing from trauma. With that being said, it's important to know that trauma doesn't just happen in childhood. It can happen throughout your life. If you had trauma as a child, that will dictate how you handle it when you're older as well. Do you need more context or information surrounding trauma? If the answer is yes, then I sincerely encourage you to purchase *Living From the Heart Jesus Gave You*. The counsel that I share with you through this study is largely based in the knowledge I have gained from my own journey, but it can be deepened through reading this excellent resource.

## Are Your Roots Rotting Your Harvest?

In my own studies, I have come across the image of trees and roots many times, and it's something that now represents a deeper concept; when images and phrases come up multiple times, it may also lead you to consider if it is a chance to stop and meditate on a deeper meaning. During an Authentic Hope support group I did with Door of Hope Ministries, they also presented this image in their manual—using trees and their roots in symbolic ways. With that in mind, try to connect the reality of trauma to the metaphor of a plant and its roots.[66] When you neglect to heal your roots, it becomes challenging to have a healthy harvest of the Fruits of the Spirit. The Bible is such an amazing resource for you through this journey to healing. Paul wrote a letter to the church in Colossae that urged them to root their very lives in their faith in Jesus Christ. Read Colossians 2:7—do you have roots that grow into your faith, or painful memories that haven't been dealt with? Paul also wrote a letter to the church in Ephesus; people have needed to be reminded of their rooted connections to God in every age. Ephesians 3:17–18 emphasizes the importance of being rooted and grounded, or healthy, in our faith.

---

66    Dale Fletcher, "Roots, Fruit, Your Heart and Your Health – Jeremiah 17:5–8," Faith and Health Connection, November 18, 2011, https://www.faithandhealthconnection.org/healthy-fruit/.

# Rotting Roots

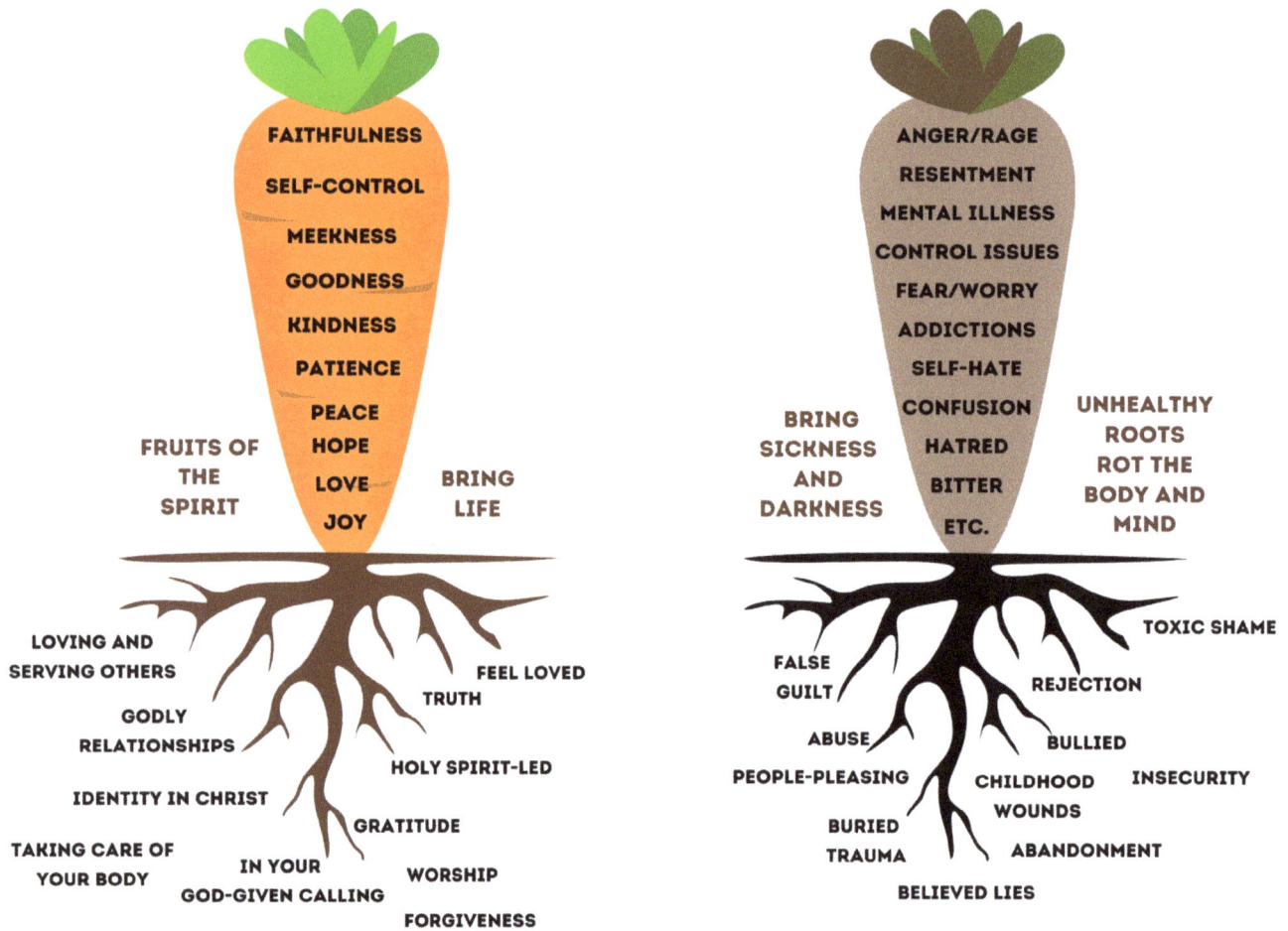

Looking at the carrot illustration is a great way to show that when you are rooted in the wrong things, your life will reflect that. Think back to the verses in Colossians and Ephesians that I just shared with you. You may need to heal your roots before you can reap the harvest God desires in your life.

Who wants to eat a rotten carrot? A horse won't, and neither will we humans! This brings me to a thought: If we are suffering and *rotting* from deeply rooted toxicity, how can we expect to reap a healthy harvest?

Rotting roots do not serve you well; they keep you stuck. When you begin to heal these roots, you can develop healthy ones and, in turn, reap a healthy harvest. Does this metaphor of roots and harvests make sense? Let's look at some tangible examples.

Have you noticed that many Christians struggle to attend church, walk away from the faith, or feel stagnant in their walk? Your roots (think of your habits and thought patterns)

cannot grow into Jesus when you are not surrounding yourself with the soil they need (think of the accountability of weekly sermons, Bible study groups, or home groups). Christians often want to please the Lord, but they are caught up in their own struggles, which make it overwhelming to be a witness for Jesus.

I can relate to this. During my health battle, I struggled to survive, let alone make a difference for God. Once I felt I had healed enough, I wanted God to use my story, so I began sharing my journey online. However, just three weeks into it, my social media account got shadow banned. There are all kinds of theories as to why shadow bans occur, but I believe it was because I was shedding light on the dangers that my past breast implants posed to my health. I was devastated; my account had begun to grow by twenty to thirty followers a day, and I was suddenly unseen. In response, I fell into a trauma response and quit sharing my story. That was when God made it clear to me that I needed more healing, specifically for my spirit and soul. Addressing my rotting roots was essential for my spiritual and emotional health, and it was a necessary step toward fulfilling God's calling on my life. I couldn't enjoy the benefits of the Fruits of the Spirit until I dealt with past and present trauma. It hasn't been an easy battle, and I'm still healing today. But God has provided me with the very tools that I am sharing with you in this book to support me along the way. What roots do you have that need healing so they can grow and yield a harvest?

# It's time for an Introduction of an

## FBEAP Philosophy

# It's Time to Introduce Another
# FBEAP – Foundational Principle:

# The Re-Circle

I want to introduce you to the next philosophy in FBEAP: the Re-Circle. This unit's topic is heavy, and trauma may be something that you feel like you can't relate to, you lie somewhere in the middle with, or you fully connect with. No matter where you fall on that spectrum, it's important to understand the philosophy of Re-Circle as you come to learn more about trauma and abuse. If you don't relate at all, you are blessed. Still, it's good to know what someone you care about may be going through. They shouldn't have to face this alone. If you do relate to the teachings, we are here to support you. You are not alone. God brought you here for a reason; He doesn't want you to feel stuck.

With how serious this topic of trauma is, it's a good time to introduce the Re-Circle. The principle of Re-Circle will help you improve the way you think about and handle the difficult situations you face.

You know I love a good illustration!

**RE-EVALUATE**

**REEVALUATE: ONCE YOU FEEL PEACE, LOOK INTO YOUR BIBLE TO SEE WHAT GOD'S WORD SAYS. PRAY TO HIM. BE STILL AND LISTEN.**

**RETREAT TO A SAFE PLACE: THE HOLY SPIRIT. HE IS WHERE WE FIND PEACE. FOCUS YOUR MIND ON HIM AND REMEMBER A JOYFUL MOMENT SPENT WITH HIM.**

**RETREAT**

**START**

**FINISH**

**RESPOND**

**RESPOND: WE CAN RETURN TO THE UNEXPECTED WHEN WE HAVE THE WISDOM WE NEED. MOVE FORWARD WITH THE HOLY SPIRIT BY YOUR SIDE!** [67]

---

[67]    Davis, *Foundations*, 26–27.

I haven't given you an example of behavior modifications that we can mimic from horses in a while! Are you ready for one now? Taking time to Re-Circle is important. When a horse feels threatened, it retreats to a safe place. From that secure location, the horse evaluates the situation and decides the best way to respond.[68] Jesus modeled this principle as well. In Matthew 26, we see that before His crucifixion, Jesus went alone to pray in the garden of Gethsemane, a safe place. There, He spent time with God, evaluating and even crying out regarding what was to come. Ultimately, He responded in the most selfless way by giving Himself so that you and I can have eternal life.

Friend, Re-Circling is essential because it allows you to have a plan in place for processing difficult situations and emotions.[69] Trauma and abuse are real and horrible aspects of life on this earth. "I have told you all this so that you may have peace in me. Here on earth you will have many trials and sorrows. But take heart, because I have overcome the world" (John 16:33). Jesus knew you would need to be rooted in Him when these words came out of His mouth. Jesus also knows that His Father has created solid and visible displays for us as we struggle through trials. Look at how God's beautiful creation—His horses—deal with fear and turmoil!

---

68    Davis and Anderson, *Gal-Up Hope Trail*, 25.
69    Davis, *Foundations*, 26–27.

# It's time for some
# Unit 4
## Check-Ins

## Check-In and Homework Time

## Part One: God Is Our Rescuer

Up until this point, unit four has walked you through two different kinds of trauma, the rotting roots that can result from those wounds, and the FBEAP principle of Re-Circling. What I am going to lead you through now is not focused on the heaviness of your trials but on the freedom that comes from your healing.

When I began my healing journey from trauma, I participated in a support group through Door of Hope Ministries that included Psalm 18. This psalm encouraged us to live victoriously and reminded us that we are not victims but victors. It profoundly impacted me, which is why I felt it was essential to include a study of Psalm 18 in this book.

Now, let's dive into Psalm 18. Note: The NIV translation will use the term *stronghold* that comes up in one of your questions.

As you reflect on Psalm 18, remember that it is a song by David. He sang these words to the Lord after He saved him from King Saul and enemies that were sent out to kill him.

**Psalm 18:1–15:**

1. After rereading verses 1–5, what speaks most to you?

2. When we think of the word *stronghold*, we often view it negatively. However, in Psalm 18, David refers to God as his *stronghold*. The only truly healthy stronghold we can have is God! Do you feel like you have unhealthy strongholds?

3. As you consider verses 4–5, when David recalls turmoil in his life, can you relate to a time when destruction seemed to surround you?

4. Look at verses 6–7. What do you think David means as he describes his crying out and the earth's response?

5. Why do you think God was angry?

6. When God showed His great power in verses 8–15, how did you feel?

**Psalm 18:16–20:**

1. What did God do for David?

2. Do you think David's enemies are spiritual enemies?

3. Do you think God knows which things are too difficult for us to handle in our own strength?

**Psalm 18:21–24:**

1. Look to verses 21–24 and meditate how you could keep the ways of the Lord.

2. Why did God reward David?

3. As you reflect on the first half of Psalm 18, what speaks to you the most? If you think that the Word of God cannot *speak* to you, then take a look at Hebrews 4:12 and then come back to this question!

## Check-In and Homework Time

## Part Two: You Can Be Victorious

**Psalm 18:25–50:**

1. Reflect on Psalm 18:25–27. What attributes of God do you hear David speak of?

2. In verses 28–31, David is so encouraging. God can turn darkness to light, His way is perfect, and He can be our rock and place of refuge. Apply these verses to your life by explaining how God has kept your lamp burning or become your rock.

3. Read through verses 32–40. How do those verses make you feel?

4. Do you see how God gave David the strength and ability to do the hard stuff?

5. What difficult challenges does God want to help you overcome?

**Psalm 18:41–50:**

1. In verses 41–50, what is David trying to convey? Remember that verse 40 refers to his enemies.

2. Why do you think David wrote Psalm 18? Why is it so important?

David was immensely thankful to God for giving him victory! As you read through the last ten verses, you can see just what God allowed His servant David to do; in one breath, the young man was singing of the weakness of his enemies and in the next of the greatness of his Lord! David wanted all who could hear to understand that true victories come from giving your whole self to God. Nothing is too big for the Lord to help you get through.

Do you know why I had you dissect Psalm 18? As I shared at the beginning of part one, I participated in a deep study of Psalm 18 myself. The *Authentic Hope Women's Support Group Manual: Healing From Abuse* by Door of Hope Ministries is an excellent resource that features similar teachings from various authors who also inspired this book. It delves deeper into the healing process from abuse, and I highly recommend participating in that study. They offer support groups that are incredibly healing.

I included this two-day study of Psalm 18 because it serves as a powerful source of inspiration that highlights that one of God's greatest servants, David, experienced abuse, accidents, illness, and various other difficulties. Yet through David's example, we learn that staying in the role of a victim isn't necessary. **With God's support, we can achieve victory.** We cannot fulfill our greatest potential while being trapped in past struggles. God desires for us to be healed.

I have given you so many questions to answer, but I want you to work through them as you travel along this pathway to healing. Friend, know that I am spurring you on through these sometimes painful questions. Let's circle back to unit four's focus!

1. Howdy! Do you feel stuck?

2. Do you feel stuck being a victim in need of rescue?

You are not alone, God is with you, and He desires for you to be healed.

## Check-In and Homework Time

## Part Three: Pushing Past Trauma That Has Trapped You

Warning! This lesson focuses on recognizing your traumas. If this feels overwhelming, please read through but feel free to skip the questions.

I felt it was important to read through Psalm 18 before working through the pressures associated with past pain. It serves as a reminder that we will face hard things, but our hope for lasting strength and healing is to lead a life guided by the Holy Spirit. With that in mind, make sure you are in a comfortable location that allows you to focus without distractions. Quiet your mind (perhaps with some of the breathing exercises I have suggested) and ask the Holy Spirit to wash His peace and wisdom over you now.

Then read through the trauma lists that are noted back toward the beginning of unit four; they may be part of Trauma A or Trauma B.

1. Are there any traumas you feel the Holy Spirit wants healed in your life?

2. Do you feel strong enough to acknowledge those feelings?

If not, that's okay; it may not be the right time. The Holy Spirit knows when we are ready. Try starting with something small rather than the bigger issues and address those first.

We want to avoid re-traumatizing anyone. If you find yourself facing traumas that feel overwhelming or if you suspect you have hidden trauma, I strongly recommend seeking help from a licensed professional counselor, ideally one who is guided by the Holy Spirit.

Remember, there's no shame in reaching out for support; I have sought counseling myself, and it's perfectly okay to get the extra help you need. Part of FBEAP is centered around herd mentality; we do not believe that you are meant to work through this life on your own but within community!

Look up the following Bible verses and reflect below:

John 16:19–24

As you navigate the healing process, it's important to use guidelines that will promote healthy roots that connect you with God's ways:

- Explore resources that can assist in the healing process. I will include some in the back of the book.

- Have reliable and supportive individuals in your life who can aid in recovering from trauma.

- Recognize the emotional patterns you may be stuck in or feelings you tend to avoid. Allow yourself to feel those emotions yet seek pathways to return to joy.

- Acknowledge the falsehoods that may creep into your wounds. Substitute those lies with the comforting truths of God. Embracing His truth can lead to your freedom!

- Take the time to pray and ask God to mend your wounds, eliminate the lies you've clung to, and fill yourself with His transformative truth. Remember, healing is a journey, and it's perfectly fine to seek support along the way.

- Don't hesitate to reach out to a professional counselor (preferably Holy Spirit-led) for assistance.

- Participate in support groups or look for prayer sessions (I will provide some options in the back of the book).

If this lesson's focus has felt overwhelming, please consider skipping the questions.

1. What are some lies that you find yourself being attacked by?

2. God loves you deeply and wants what is best for you. Do you believe that? Look up and reflect on the verses below:

   Jeremiah 29:10—11          Zephaniah 3:17          James 1:1-8

I think it would be beneficial to do an exercise so that you can identify some of those rotten roots in your life.

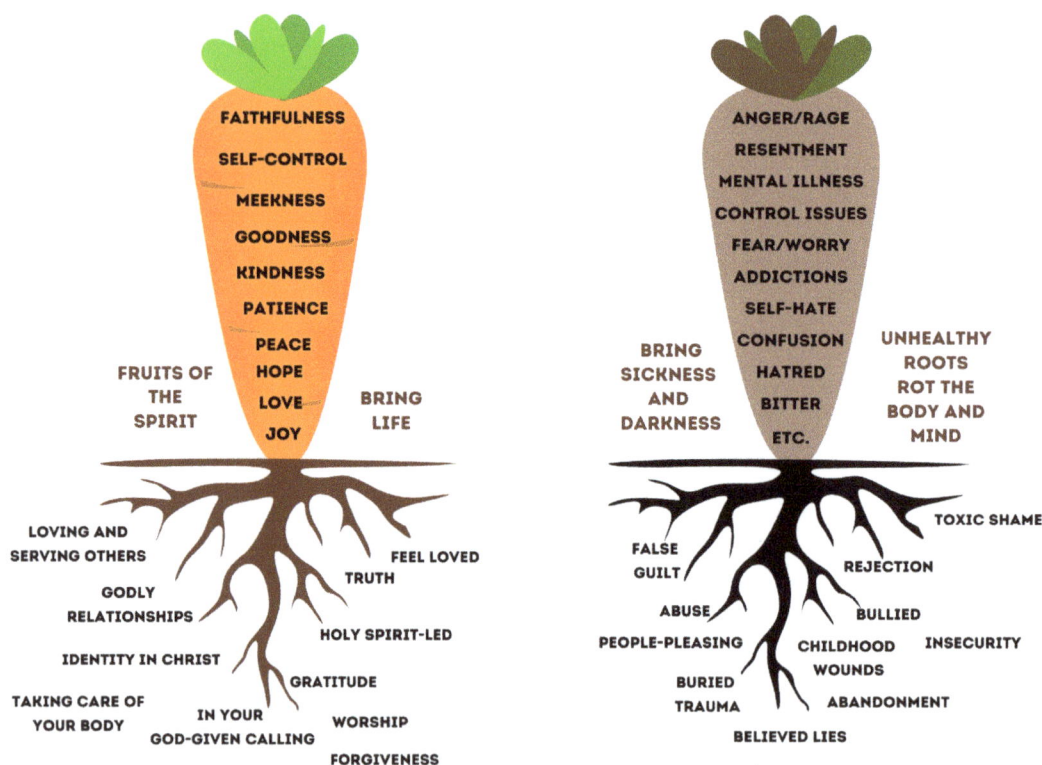

Up above on the rotting carrot, circle what you can relate to. Getting to the bottom of those roots can help bring freedom and healing!

Next, circle your goals on the healthy carrot. Also, look at the phrases surrounding the healthy roots and circle what you can do to start healing *your* roots. Take time with the Holy Spirit; He will reveal what you can do![70]

---

70      Fletcher, "Roots, Fruit, Your Heart and Your Health – Jeremiah 17:5–8."

## Checking In on FBEAP – Foundational Principle: The Re-Circle

At the beginning of this unit, you read "Howdy! Are You Stuck?" You may not have realized how hard it could be to talk about being stuck by trauma, but I truly hope that focusing on the FBEAP of Re-Circling allowed you to take it all in stride.

Are you good at knowing when to step away and go to a safe place to process challenging things with the Lord? Hopefully, working through the questions that I posed to you in this unit have started you on a path that ends in a "Yes, I am!"

We all respond more healthily when we invite the Holy Spirit to calm us and incorporate His Word into our responses. Are you skilled at delving into the Word of God—the Bible—to seek guidance?

I hope that this unit wasn't too challenging for you. Trauma can be a painful subject. However, when left unaddressed, it can cause harmful issues. Remember, healing is a journey, not a sprint. Now that you are more informed about trauma, you can start to work on healing your wounds. And if you feel like you don't have much or any trauma, you can be a sound mentor and friend to those who need a mature person to help them recover. It's important that everyone learns about trauma so we can have a strong, healthy herd!

# Prayers and Praises

*It's time for*

# Unit 5

## Say Howdy to Healthy Coping!

# Say Howdy to Healthy Coping!

Before you fully understand healthy coping techniques, you may need to first consider if you are already using unhealthy ones. What is an unhealthy coping mechanism? It's a learned behavior that most likely developed in childhood as a way to deal with stress and pain. Poor coping mechanisms don't resolve issues, and the wounded individual struggles to regain stability.[71] Here are some examples below:

- Individuals may isolate themselves and reject help from others.
- They often rationalize peers' inappropriate behaviors.
- A person may appear happy externally while feeling dissatisfied internally.
- Excusing unacceptable behavior can weaken personal boundaries.
- Many choose denial for a sense of security.
- People frequently blame others instead of acknowledging their own mistakes.
- A fantasy world may be created, providing more satisfaction than reality.
- Emotions can be projected onto others.
- Attacking others can serve to maintain distance.
- Difficult conversations may be avoided.
- The tendency to rescue others can distract from personal challenges (people-pleasing).
- Emotional eating may arise as a coping mechanism.
- Struggles with addiction and self-harm may occur.
- Negative self-talk can lead to feelings of inadequacy.
- Avoidance behaviors may surface in response to challenges.
- Procrastination can become common.
- Overworking can serve as a distraction from underlying issues.

---

71    "Identifying Unhealthy Coping Mechanisms," Seattle Christian Counseling, April 28, 2021, https://seattlechristiancounseling.com/articles/identifying-unhealthy-coping-mechanisms.

# What Approach Am I Operating In?

As an introverted person who cherishes quiet alone time, I have many days when I would prefer to avoid approaching others or dealing with certain issues. However, life does not always allow for that. We inevitably encounter people and problems that need our attention. A key aspect of healthy coping is recognizing how we navigate relationships. Using an unhealthy approach can negatively affect our mental and spiritual well-being. It is easy to fall into unproductive patterns. Also, knowing what approaches people use can help identify whether healthy boundaries need to be established with that person.

Inspired by the book *The Other Half of Church*, this section emphasizes the importance of being mindful in our relationships and recognizing when we need to improve our behaviors.[72] At Our Healing Farm, we use memorable terms: the Outlaw Approach, the Scoundrel Approach, and the Partner Approach. The choice of these Western-themed names is intentional; they serve as easy-to-remember reminders during conflict that help you identify what approach you are using and reflect on your own or another's behavior. This reflection may reveal that you act like an Outlaw or even a Scoundrel. Still, by recognizing this, you can work on resetting your relational circuits, finding healing, and fostering peace in your relationships.[73]

**OUTLAW APPROACH**

*Outlaw* means "opponent." This approach occurs when your defenses are up and you react or don't react in a productive way. In this approach, your relational circuits are off. You may choose to check out, not wanting to listen, lose your temper, become judgmental, and maybe even want to go into fix-it-now mode.[74] We all can operate in Outlaw Approach, and it's good that we become aware of when we are in it.

When a person is in Scoundrel Approach, their relational circuits are very much turned on but not for the right reasons—in this approach, the person wants to win and control at any cost and makes excuses for poor choices, and this is where narcissistic behaviors come out to play.[75]

**SCOUNDREL APPROACH**

In my healing and witnessing others heal, I have seen that operating in a Scoundrel Approach can involve unresolved wounds, which can reveal the need for healing. It can also be an attack from spiritual warfare. Remember when we talked about who and what we can hang our hat on

---

72    Wilder and Hendricks, *The Other Half of Church*, 155–79, 223–24.
73    Wilder and Hendricks, *The Other Half of Church*, 187–94.
74    Wilder and Hendricks, *The Other Half of Church*, 223.
75    Wilder and Hendricks, *The Other Half of Church*, 155–79, 223–24.

or with? The Enemy can use our wounds and attack us. We have the authority to pray against spiritual warfare that may be attacking us and also work on our healing, so in return, we don't act like Scoundrels ourselves!

**PARTNER APPROACH**

When I think of a Partner, I envision someone who genuinely cares for me—someone who is willing to walk beside me through good times and bad. They don't just listen; they hear me and are committed to building something real and lasting. A strong relationship is built on trust, effort, and shared purpose.

We should aspire to adopt a Partner Approach in our relationships. Our focus should be on genuinely caring about the other person's feelings and maintaining a loving, protective, and engaged state.[76]

## There Is Hope!

We can step out of an Outlaw Approach by reconnecting our relational circuits, meeting with sound mentors, and inviting God into the situation. We move away from Scoundrel Approach by finding empathy for our perceived adversaries, praying for them,[77] and praying against spiritual warfare attacking us when needed. We also need to remember that sometimes healthy boundaries are needed when dealing with Scoundrels with narcissistic behaviors.

---

76    Wilder and Hendricks, *The Other Half of Church*, 224.
77    Wilder and Hendricks, *The Other Half of Church*, 187–94.

# Riding the Trail to Healing

**TRAIL OF TOXICITY**

STUCK AND LOST ON THE TRAIL

POOR COPING

FEEL DOWN AND OPPRESSED

BELIEVE THE ENEMY'S LIES

FEEL UNWORTHY

YOU ARE HURT

JESUS GOT LEFT BEHIND

**STABLE (JOY)**
NEED TO GET BACK TO JOY

**TRAIL OF HEALING**

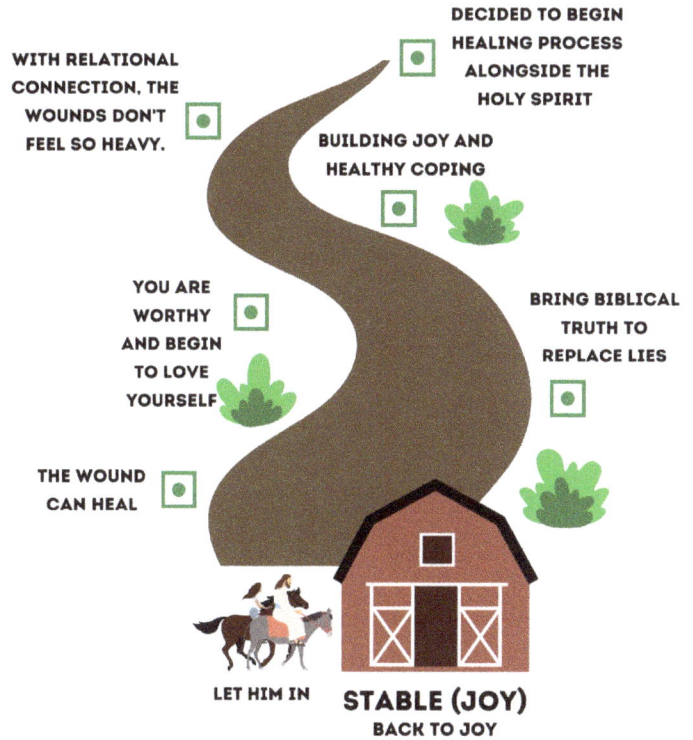

DECIDED TO BEGIN HEALING PROCESS ALONGSIDE THE HOLY SPIRIT

WITH RELATIONAL CONNECTION, THE WOUNDS DON'T FEEL SO HEAVY.

BUILDING JOY AND HEALTHY COPING

YOU ARE WORTHY AND BEGIN TO LOVE YOURSELF

BRING BIBLICAL TRUTH TO REPLACE LIES

THE WOUND CAN HEAL

LET HIM IN

**STABLE (JOY)**
BACK TO JOY

Take a moment to think back to unit four, where you dealt with past trauma or perhaps just learned about it. Saying howdy to healthy coping might require that you actively pursue new behaviors and thought patterns. We often resort to unhealthy coping mechanisms and may find ourselves following a trail of toxicity because we carry emotional wounds. Is this something you can see in your own life? In this illustration, I want to highlight the differences between unhealthy and healthy trails. Riding the trail to healing requires *commitment to healing*, and it is essential to change the unhealthy habits that need to be altered.

Are you saying, "Well, great! But how do I start?"

# Howdy! Let's Do a Round-Up!

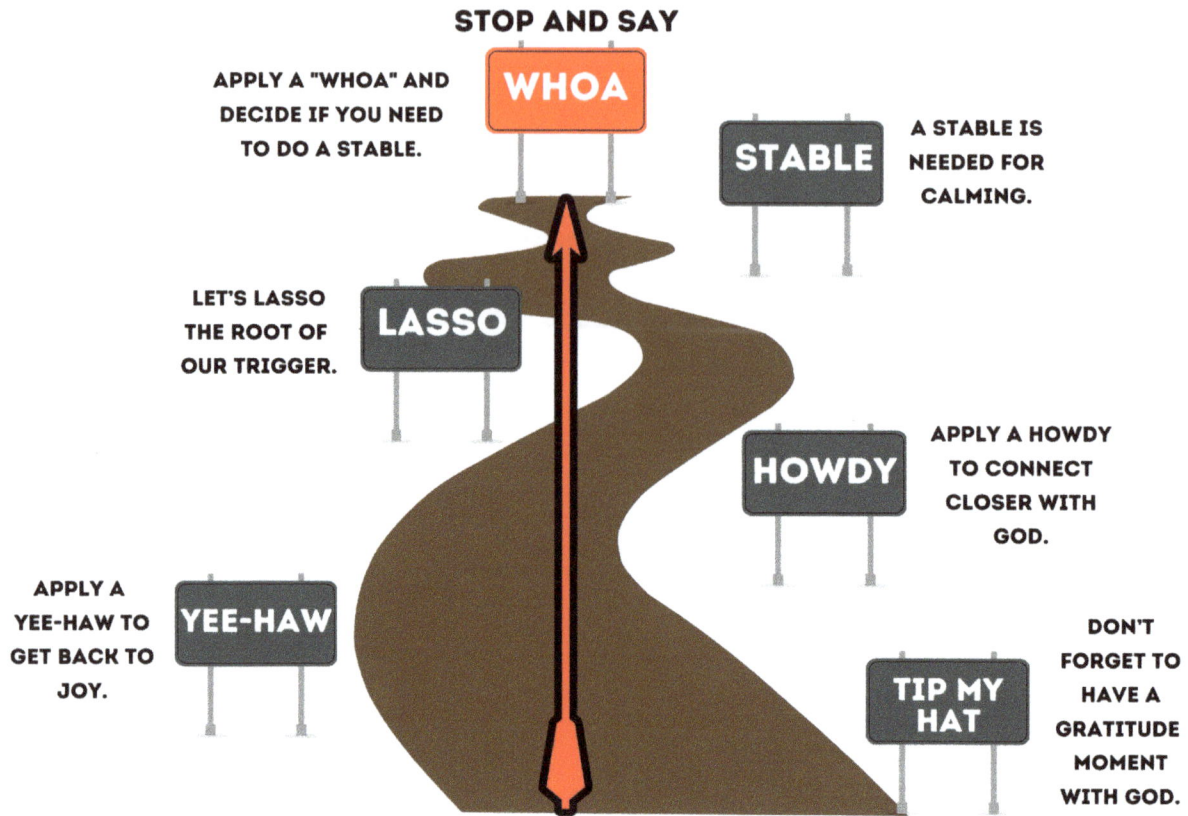

**STOP AND SAY**

**WHOA**

APPLY A "WHOA" AND DECIDE IF YOU NEED TO DO A STABLE.

**STABLE**

A STABLE IS NEEDED FOR CALMING.

LET'S LASSO THE ROOT OF OUR TRIGGER.

**LASSO**

**HOWDY**

APPLY A HOWDY TO CONNECT CLOSER WITH GOD.

APPLY A YEE-HAW TO GET BACK TO JOY.

**YEE-HAW**

**TIP MY HAT**

DON'T FORGET TO HAVE A GRATITUDE MOMENT WITH GOD.

**THE FEELING OF BEING TRIGGERED**

We all experience triggers at some point in our lives; it's not a matter of if, but when. Part of the healing process involves understanding the root causes of these triggers and working toward returning to a healthier state. In the following pages, I will further elaborate on the concepts of the Round-Up: WHOA, STABLE, LASSO, HOWDY, and YEEHAW.

When you face a trigger or something that brings up trauma or even mental health issues, you may think, *I don't want to act like this!* This is the perfect moment to ask yourself a question that we use at Our Healing Farm.

## "Am I Acting Howdy or Rowdy?"

When you hear the word *Howdy,* what comes to mind? For me, it evokes feelings that are friendly, positive, and a little silly. On the other hand, when you think of *Rowdy,* what do you think of? Perhaps it evokes thoughts of being out of control, loud, anxious, annoyed, and disorderly. In this way, I want you to understand that *Howdy* represents positivity while *Rowdy* signifies negativity.

In your daily life, you can choose to respond positively or negatively to the challenges you face. You have the option to adopt life-giving or life-sucking coping mechanisms. A more lighthearted way to become more aware of our thoughts and behaviors is to ask ourselves, "Is my mind thinking *Howdy* or *Rowdy* right now?"

Let's pull this explanation back to horses—they are such amazing teachers. Now, imagine a situation where a horse is being rowdy while you are riding it. What do you do? You pull back and say, "WHOA." With that in mind, I would like to introduce the WHOA as a way to help manage our actions and reactions (coping).

## The WHOA!

"Understand this, my dear brothers and sisters: You must all be quick to listen, slow to speak, and slow to get angry" (James 1:19).

**W** WAIT BEFORE RESPONDING. CONSIDER WHETHER YOU'RE BEING HOWDY OR ROWDY. ARE YOU TRIGGERED?

**H** HOLY SPIRIT. LISTEN FOR HIS SOFT VOICE. PRAY.

**O** OBSERVE HOW YOU ARE FEELING.

**A** ACTION MAY BE NEEDED. CHOOSE IF YOU NEED TO GET STABLE (THINK BACK TO THE IMAGE FROM THE TRAIL TO HEALING) OR IF YOU ARE IN A HEALTHY PLACE TO RESPOND.

Whenever you feel the urge to use an unhealthy coping strategy, whether you're about to lose your temper or have already done so, take a moment to reflect on your approach. Is it a Howdy mindset (positive) or a Rowdy mindset (negative)? Consider whether you need to apply a WHOA to pause and seek guidance from the Holy Spirit in order to make a better choice.

This next concept doesn't include a clever acronym, but I believe the Lord has put it on my heart and mind to share within the pages of this book with you.

## Bridle Your Tongue

Why can it be so hard to say, "WHOA!" in your daily life?

If you're anything like me—an imperfect soul—you may struggle with saying, "WHOA." At times, emotions can hit hard and leave you feeling like a failure because it's challenging to control them.

That was my experience for most of my adult life until I was introduced to The Life Model. Difficulty in managing our words or actions often stems from buried trauma, which leads to poor coping mechanisms. However, it can also arise from neglecting our spiritual and physical bodies, which are temples of the Holy Spirit (1 Corinthians 6:19).

**Bridling** the *Tongue* so you can say **WHOA** *Requires* living Holy Spirit-led.

I mention this because without taking time for resets—like calming our bodies, practicing gratitude, sparking joy, caring for our physical health, healing our emotional roots, taking authority over spiritual warfare, and nurturing our relationships with God and others—we won't be able to easily say, "WHOA."

I found that I could better manage my reactions and bridle my tongue when I prioritized seeking spiritual, physical, and mental healing, worked on my personal maturity, and changed my habits to include living a Holy Spirit-led life.

I'm not perfect and still have my mess-up moments when I have difficulty saying, "WHOA," which is normal, but I'm growing, and they are happening much less.

Take a look at these two verses; both James (Jesus's brother) and King Solomon wrote on the concept of bridling one's tongue!

"If anyone thinks he is religious and does not bridle his tongue but deceives his heart, this person's religion is worthless" (James 1:26 ESV).

"Whoever derides their neighbor has no sense, but the one who has understanding holds their tongue" (Proverbs 11:12 NIV).

Bridling the tongue so you can say, "WHOA" requires living a Holy Spirit-led life!

# The STABLE Method

Here is another acronym for you all! Hopefully having these terms will help you as you journey along the trail to healing! Applying the STABLE method aims to bring calm to your body and mind. I want to draw attention to the fight-flight-freeze response, a stress reaction that enables you to respond to perceived dangers, such as suddenly needing to stop a car or feeling threatened while walking down the street. Occasionally, the fight-flight-freeze response becomes overly sensitive when your nervous system is heightened. This occurs when harmless situations activate the response. Heightened responses are more prevalent in individuals who have undergone trauma.

Unfortunately, I dealt with having an overactive response for years. Having tools to cope better is essential, so the STABLE method was born. I adapted this method from some of the teachings in *The 4 Habits of Joy-Filled People*.[78] I want to emphasize that experiencing dysregulated responses is normal, even daily, as we are all imperfect humans. Adopting the STABLE method can help you improve your habits and achieve a healthier state. This process requires you to retrain yourself by replacing old habits with new ones. The Holy Spirit is eager to assist you in this journey. Once you reach a calmer and more stable state, you will be better equipped to process your next actions.

**S** SAFE PLACE, AS IN GO TO A SAFE PLACE AND LET YOURSELF FEEL THE EMOTIONS.

**T** TAKE A MOMENT TO RESET YOUR BRAIN THROUGH BREATHING, GRATITUDE, OR WORSHIP MUSIC.

**A** ASK FOR THE HOLY SPIRIT'S HELP IN UNDERSTANDING HOW YOU ARE FEELING.

**B** BRING TRUTH TO YOUR EMOTIONS; LOOK UP SCRIPTURE ON HOW YOU ARE FEELING

**L** LIST WAYS YOU CAN BETTER MOVE FORWARD: DO A LASSO, HOWDY, AND YEEHAW OR SEEK HELP.

**E** END IN A CALMER STATE.

---

78    Warner and Coursey, *The 4 Habits of Joy-Filled People*, 49–58.

# The LASSO Method

Do you remember, way back in unit four, reading about rotten roots that can steal your fruit? Identifying the root of your triggers is essential for healing the wound. Once you feel stable, it's a great opportunity to explore why you were triggered in the first place. If you believe you are strong enough, using a technique like the LASSO can be helpful in uncovering the true reason behind a behavior. The Holy Spirit can assist you in lassoing the root of a trigger—just ask for guidance. Take time to be still with the Holy Spirit and ask Him to help you understand the root of why you are really triggered.

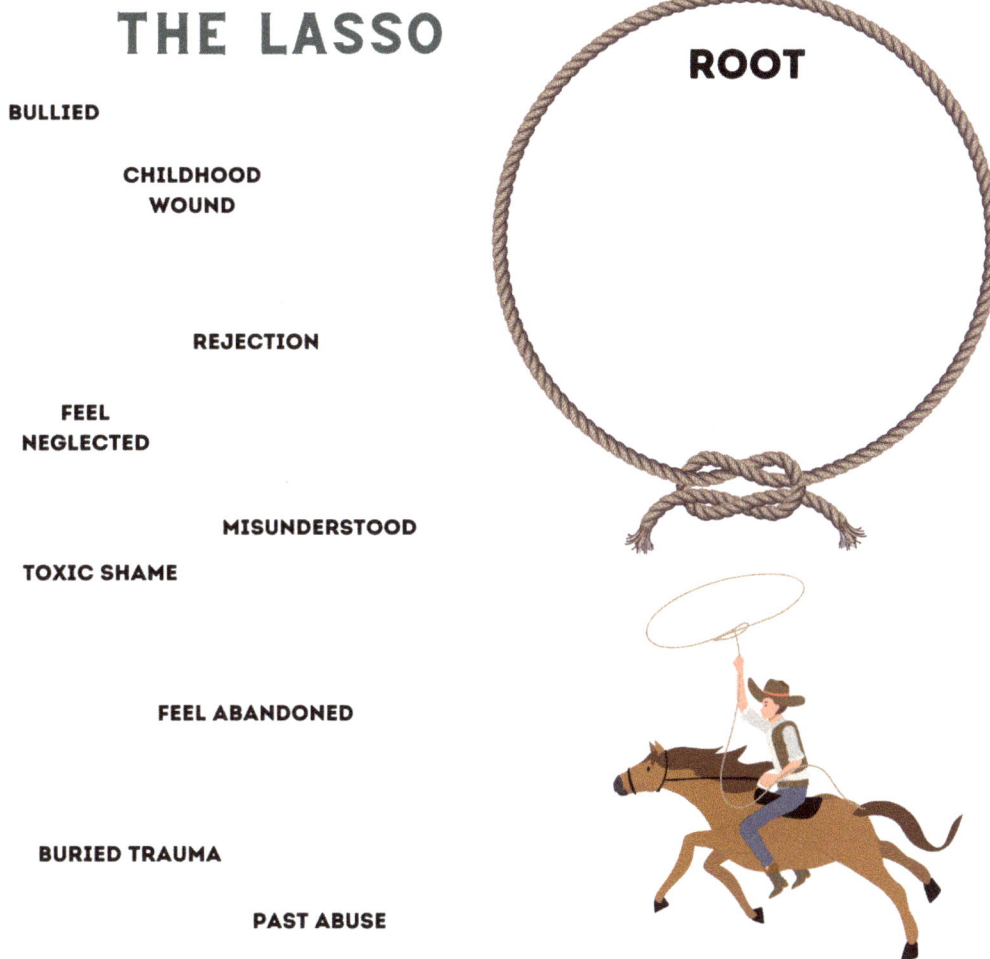

## THE LASSO

ROOT

BULLIED

CHILDHOOD
WOUND

REJECTION

FEEL
NEGLECTED

MISUNDERSTOOD

TOXIC SHAME

FEEL ABANDONED

BURIED TRAUMA

PAST ABUSE

While you may have experience with horses, you may not have experience with a lasso. Despite your level of expertise here, I'm sure you can recall a Western movie or rodeo show as you visualize just what the lasso can do. It is amazing that a rope can be used to bring an animal that is four times that of a human into submission. Think of that as you imagine lassoing your trauma or emotions.

Once you have lassoed your root, take a moment to pray and ask God for guidance in becoming more aware of this trigger and for assistance in healing the pain associated with it. You might also consider seeking help from a licensed counselor to support you in addressing and healing deeper-rooted issues.

## The HOWDY Method

I shared this method with you all way back in unit one! For the sake of putting all of the healthy coping strategies together, I'm including it for you again here!

**H** — HOLY SPIRIT TIME! TAKE TIME TO BE STILL, PRAY, AND LISTEN.

*"Howdy, Holy Spirit..."*

**O** — OBSERVE AND WRITE WHAT YOU ARE HEARING AND FEELING.

**W** — WHAT DOES GOD'S WORD SAY? READ AND REFLECT ON SCRIPTURE.

**D** — DISCOVER (ASK, SEEK, AND WRITE) WHAT THE HOLY SPIRIT HAS FOR YOU TO DO TODAY!

**Y** — YES! YOU CAN DO WHAT HE LEADS YOU TO ACCOMPLISH!

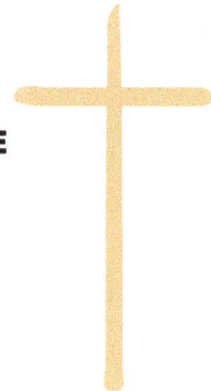

*Don't forget to give prayer requests and praises!*

Friend, don't forget to give your prayer requests and praises! The best habit we can have is checking in daily with the Holy Spirit! Struggling? Use a HOWDY to help you get connected to God!

## The YEEHAW

I recently learned that the term *yeehaw* is a way to express joy, and it really resonated with me.[79] I understand that life can get busy and overwhelming, so I've found it helpful to think of fun ways to reconnect with joy. Now, when I feel down, I can ask myself if I need a YEEHAW moment to lift my spirits and get back to a place of joy. Some of these realizations have come from reading *The Other Half of Church*,[80] but this helpful acronym is something we have developed at Our Healing Farm.

**Y** — YOU CAN FIND JOY.
TELL YOURSELF THAT!

**E** — ENGAGE WITH THE HOLY SPIRIT.
BE STILL AND LISTEN.

**E** — ENCOURAGE YOURSELF TO RECALL A JOYFUL
MOMENT OF GRATITUDE FROM YOUR MEMORY.

**H** — HOLD ONTO THAT MOMENT AS LONG
AS YOU CAN, UP TO FIVE MINUTES.

**A** — ASSESS HOW YOU FEEL IN YOUR
MIND AND BODY.

**W** — WELCOME THE FEELING OF JOY
AND GIVE THE LORD GRATITUDE.

Try to repeat this one to three times a day.

---

79    Dictionary.com, s.v. "Yeehaw (*n.*)," accessed September 17, 2025, https://www.dictionary.com/browse/yeehaw.

80    Hendricks and Wilder, *The Other Half of Church*, 217–20.

## Tip My Hat

After reading the book *Joyful Journey: Listening to Immanuel*, I felt led to add in another method to the Round-Up.[81] I adapted this method from their writing, and it's called Tip My Hat.

In the Western world, when a cowboy felt deep gratitude, he would tip his hat and say, "Much obliged!" Remembering to tip your hat to Jesus every day with a moment of gratitude is so important. It's not only good for growing your joy center, but it's good for strengthening your relationship with the Lord!

**The Method:**

TIP YOUR HAT to Jesus and say, "Much obliged!"

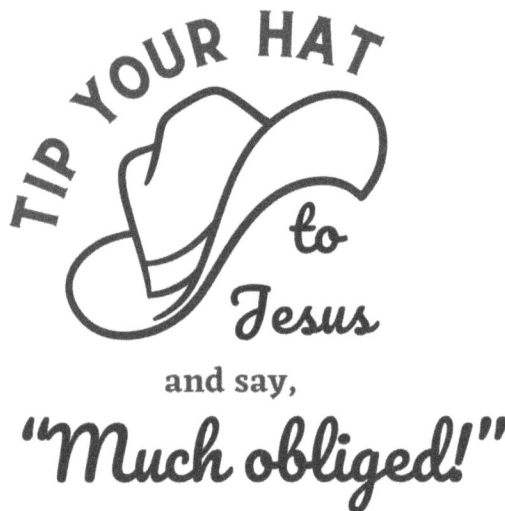

**BE STILL WITH THE HOLY SPIRIT AND ASK HIM TO GIVE YOU A MEMORY THAT YOU ARE THANKFUL FOR.**

**WRITE THAT MEMORY OUT AND THANK GOD FOR IT!**

**TAKE TIME TO WRITE WHAT YOU THINK GOD IS SHOWING YOU THROUGH THAT EXPERIENCE.**

**CAN YOU CONNECT THIS MOMENT TO A SPECIFIC SCRIPTURE? IF SO, MAKE A NOTE OF THAT ALSO.**

**SIT STILL AND ALLOW YOURSELF TO FEEL GRATEFUL FOR THAT EXPERIENCE!**

**TIP YOUR HAT TO JESUS ONCE A DAY!**

---

81     E. James Wilder et al., *Joyful Journey: Listening to Immanuel* (Life Model Works™, 2015), 21–24.

## Take Time to Gather Up!

The book *Joyful Journey: Listening to Immanuel* emphasizes the importance of sharing our relational experiences with those around us. Doing so builds our relationships with each other and strengthens our connection to the Lord, ultimately enriching our joy centers. God created us to be relational and to share our lives with others. Taking the time to express our Round-Ups, especially our YEEHAW and Tip My Hat moments, brings joy to one another and peace to our souls.

# It's time for an Introduction of an FBEAP Philosophy

# It's Time to Introduce Another FBEAP – Foundational Principle:

# Push/Pull

This week, I want to teach you about another principle from FBEAP, specifically the concept of Push/Pull. It's a great time to introduce it as we are looking at how we are coping with experiences in our lives. I made an illustration to help explain it!

Pushing into the harness allows the horse to create the strongest force of movement. When you and I push forward, we are focusing on what's ahead just as the horse does.

While it may make sense that pushing creates movement, it is important to remember that pulling can do the same thing. As a rider pulls back on the reins of a horse, that initiates a change in movement. Pulling back is beneficial for initiating movement with machinery as well; just think of starting a lawnmower or weed whacker. However, pulling demands significantly more energy than pushing, which can make you feel weak. It can also hinder movement or even leave you stuck or moving backward.

As you continue your healing journey, I encourage you to pay attention to whether you are pushing forward toward healing or engaging in more pulling movements. It's okay to pull back at first to assess what is happening, but remember to push forward again toward healing. Just like horses that may initially pull back, the ultimate goal is to move forward toward safety. As humans, we will naturally experience both pushing and pulling as these movements are essential. However, I want you to focus more on pushing as it is the more powerful movement.[82]

---

82    Davis, *Foundations*, 30–31.

# It's time for some
## Unit 5
## Check-Ins

★ ★ ★

# Check-In and Homework Time

## Part One: What Is Ruling Your Mind?

Many people have developed an unhealthy relationship with themselves. To cultivate a healthy self-relationship, you must align with God's perspective on your worth. This alignment allows you to embrace His truth and genuinely care for yourself.

Your thoughts, toxic shame, distorted guilt, and the burdens you choose to carry can significantly affect how you view yourself. The mind can feel like a very chaotic place, like a wild rodeo. When this is happening, it makes it challenging to discern the truth. This is why you must protect your mind by staying aware of what is happening within your mind, body, and spirit. Remember that God doesn't want you to carry thoughts or burdens that are not yours to bear.

Let's explore this wild rodeo of the mind and reflect on the things that do not serve you well. It's important to remind yourself, *Not my rodeo; not my bull or bronc.*

If I asked you to hop on a raging bull or bronc without any training, would you do it? Would you even go near one? Probably not, because you know it's dangerous. Bronc and bull riders have years of experience. So why do we let mental bulls and broncs dominate our minds? We shouldn't. God wants us to be healthy, not to be caught in the wild ride created by the Enemy or others. If you are distracted by the turmoil in your mind, you will not be focused on what God wants you to do.

Do you hold onto shame? Are you taking on burdens that aren't yours to bear? Do you find yourself people-pleasing to avoid confrontation, which leaves you feeling exhausted? Or are you the type of person who feels the need to fix everything and everyone? Perhaps distorted guilt makes you feel stuck. All of this is fueled by the Enemy's lies or the opinions and actions of others. But guess what? God doesn't tear you down; He inspires and builds you up. While God can see our sins, the blood of Jesus has made them as white as snow. It's the Enemy who seeks to bring you down and to fill your mind with doubt, fear, and discouragement. You don't have to stay on a wild ride; you can heal alongside Jesus!

★ ★ ★

# Not my

## Rodeo
### not my Bull or Bronc ...

## PEOPLE-PLEASER

These people feel the need to make everyone happy and do not stand up for themselves. Remember, God didn't make you to be a doormat.

## PEOPLE-FIXER

These individuals believe they can and should fix others; you are not in charge of fixing people—God is. Others have to want to fix themselves.

## TOXIC SHAME

Self-hate, feelings of unworthiness, and an inability to forgive yourself can be fed by the Enemy or others.

## DISTORTED GUILT

Distorted guilt can happen even after you have truly repented and received forgiveness from the Lord for your sins. The Enemy may still plant seeds of shame that lead you to feel inadequate or like a failure.

## ENEMY'S LIES

The Enemy will fill your head with lies to distract you; just look at John 8:44.

83, 84

83     Jared Mellinger, "Fighting False Guilt," New Growth Press (blog), August 8, 2022, https://blog.new-growthpress.com/fighting-false-guilt/#:~:text=False%20guilt%20has%20a%20strong,others%20thinking%20less%20of%20us.

84     "What Is Toxic Shame?," WebMD, February 25, 2024, https://www.webmd.com/mental-health/what-is-toxic-shame.

# How Can You Get Off the Wild Ride?

## Have Grit!

At Our Healing Farm, having grit means finding courage and strength from the Lord and perseverance that comes through a close relationship with Him to achieve healing. Bring shame, distorted guilt, and battles you are fighting out of the darkness and into the light. They thrive in hiding but cannot survive when exposed. Attempting to bury your battles only causes them to grow. Discussing or reflecting on what causes your struggles may be painful at first, but it will ultimately reduce those feelings. If you don't have a sound person (think back to unit two) in your life to share with, consider writing down your feelings to the Lord. Having grit also means taking authority against the Enemy, who may be filling your head with lies. God has given us the authority to give the Enemy the boot!

## Build Your Joy Center

Focus on filling your joy center capacity, as we learned about in the "Say Howdy and Spark Some Joy!" unit. Remember, we can always grow our joy centers. It's never too late to build joy and store it in our brains. This will help you overcome toxic shame and false guilt.

Be mindful of joy robbers. The Enemy will attempt to steal your joy through shame, guilt, worry, fear, and especially the actions of others. I have experienced times when I felt surrounded by attacks that robbed me of my ability to find joy. To combat this, you need grit—determination to seek out true joy rather than settling for fake joy. This might require a real struggle of the flesh to overcome the urge to wallow in bed when finding joy feels impossible. I've been there. It might take all the strength you have to get back to finding joy during such battles, but don't give up! Stay determined to use the positive coping strategies you've learned from this book and turn to godly things that truly work. Keep pushing forward, even when all you feel is pain, until you achieve a breakthrough victory. Remember, it's in the trials that God grows us the most. He can bring joy during sorrow if we look for it and let Him.

## What's Your Verse?

The phrase "What's your verse?" is inspired by LeEtta Rose Darcy. When her loved ones approached her to share their struggles, she offered them comfort while also asking, "What's your verse?" This encouraged them to turn to God's Word, as He is our true comforter and problem solver. Always turn to Scripture for truth and guidance. You can't go wrong with that.

YOU MAY THINK,

> I'M UNWORTHY.        I'M UNLOVEABLE.
>
> I CAN'T DO IT.    I CAN'T TAKE ANYMORE.
>
> I'M ALWAYS WORRYING.      I FEEL ALONE.
>
> I'M FORGIVEABLE.      I'M NOT SMART .

## BUT...

## REMEMBER THIS....

> "I HAVE NOT GIVEN YOU A SPIRIT OF FEAR."
>
> "I LOVE YOU."    "YOU CAN DO ALL THINGS."
>
> "I WILL NEVER LEAVE OR FORSAKE YOU."
>
> "I WILL SUPPLY ALL YOUR NEEDS."
>
> "I GIVE YOU WISDOM."
>
> "CAST YOUR CARES UPON ME."

## What's your verse?

## Prayer and Prayer Partners

Prayer is vital to a close, Holy Spirit-led relationship. As you can see in the Round-Up process, each step encourages leaning into prayer. Connecting with God through prayer is a lifeline for me. He is the best encourager and comforter.

But what about those times when it feels hard to pray? Things have spiraled, or the attacks are so heavy that you feel as if you cannot do it alone. Remember our lesson on having a herd? When I have been under some of my most brutal attacks, I have had to fight my flesh to battle alone and reach out for sound prayer partners to help pray and encourage me through the fight.

Have you ever heard the term *ponying*? Ponying horses is the practice of leading one horse while riding another, and it often plays a crucial role in helping younger, inexperienced, or anxious horses stay calm and focused—especially in high-stress situations like heading to the starting gate at a racetrack. In fact, it's common to see seasoned pony horses with riders calmly guiding racehorses who might otherwise act up or resist going where they need to go. Sometimes the horse being ponied even has a rider on it—someone needing help getting their mount settled enough to move forward safely. In much the same way, we all face moments in life where we need someone to be ponying us to a place of calm and assurance—someone to ride with us through a hard season, helping us focus, praying with us, and encouraging us when we can't quite do it alone. Just like a pony horse helps another horse reach the destination with a steadier heart and mind, God often uses people in our lives to lead us with gentleness and strength, especially when the path ahead feels overwhelming. This has happened to me often, friend, when life throws overwhelming and stressful situations at me, and I have to fight my flesh and reach out for a sound person to help pony me back to a functioning state. Remember, we are meant to be like a herd and not walk through hard stuff alone. Struggling? Reach out for someone to help guide you and pray with you so that you can have victory!

## Free Yourself, Friend—Forgive

"Forgiveness" is such a touchy word. Believe me, I know.

I've been hurt deeply by others—wounds that left behind real trauma. The bitterness, the anger, the pain . . . it can all take over my mind until it's hard to function, let alone live the way I know God wants me to.

For years, I struggled to understand what forgiveness really meant. To me, it felt like giving someone a free pass. Can you relate?

But over time, I learned something that changed my perspective:

- Forgiveness means giving the person to God in prayer. It's a way to still walk in love, even with someone who's hurt you.

- It means letting go of your need for revenge. Justice belongs to God—and He will handle it perfectly.

- It means setting healthy boundaries. Kindness doesn't always mean being "nice." Sometimes it just means being civil—without allowing someone unsafe back into your inner life. And if that person isn't safe, no contact is okay.

- And most importantly: Reconciliation is not the same as forgiveness. Reconciliation only happens when the offender truly repents and shows consistent, lasting change.

Forgiveness is about releasing that person into God's hands. It's how we protect our minds and hearts from being ruled by unhealthy emotions and coping mechanisms.

And sometimes? You have to forgive again and again. That's what Jesus meant when He said we're to forgive "seventy times seven." Especially when you're dealing with repeat offenders or deep, painful triggers, you may find yourself giving the same situation to God over and over. And that's okay. He sees your heart, and He honors your obedience.

Forgiving someone doesn't erase the pain. It doesn't excuse what happened. But it does open the door for God to bring you peace—the kind of peace that only He can give.

## Letting Go of Shame and Guilt

1. As you read through this lesson, can you relate to being on a wild rodeo ride in your mind?

2. What are some unhealthy thought patterns you find yourself struggling with?

3. Look up Psalm 147:3. How does it connect to the idea of a "wild ride" or even to healthy coping techniques you've learned about in unit five?

4. Can you relate to distorted guilt and toxic shame? If so, why do you feel like you can't be forgiven?

5. Look up 1 John 1:9. How does this verse connect to this lesson on healthy coping?

It is so encouraging to know that the Lord wants you and me to be free from fear and shame! He desires for us to live a life filled with joy! Before you begin your prayers and praises, meditate on the psalm below.

> "I prayed to the LORD, and he answered me. He freed me from all my fears. Those who look to him for help will be radiant with joy; no shadow of shame" (Psalm 34:4–5).

## What's Your Verse?

1. Do you do well at turning to Scripture when things feel tough?

Here's a fun fact: In the Bible app, when you navigate to the Bible section, you can use the magnifying glass icon to search for keywords related to your feelings. This feature brings up Sriptures that address those topics. It's been really helpful in my life!

## Prayer Is Powerful

1. When your mind feels like it's on a wild ride, do you take a moment to pray?

2. Do you believe that prayer can bring supernatural peace?

I know that it can be challenging to find the words to pray during tough times. Do you have a sound prayer partner you can reach out to?

When I have experienced deep pain, my prayer partners help me through the battles when I lack strength. Their support brings peace amidst the chaos.

    3. Do you have any sound prayer partners?

If not, let's pray now that God brings someone into your life.

## Forgiving Is Freeing

    1. Is there someone you're struggling to forgive?

    2. Does the thought of letting it go feel impossible?

That's the enemy's trap—whispering lies that say you can't forgive, that you have to hold onto resentment to stay strong. But that lie keeps you stuck. It hijacks your healing.

Listen, forgiveness doesn't mean the pain goes away overnight. It means you're no longer carrying it alone. You're putting it in God's hands—where it belongs.

Let Him be the one to deal with justice. Let Him bring you peace.

    3. Is there someone God is asking you to release to Him today?

Take a moment—just between you and God—and do that now.

I know that wasn't easy. And I know the pain might still be there.

So tell God about it. Be honest. Ask Him to comfort you in that space.

Releasing others to God is one of the healthiest things you can do for your mind, your heart, and your soul.

## Check-In and Homework Time

## Part Two: Coping Mechanisms

1.  What unhealthy coping mechanisms can you relate to?



2. Do you believe that the Lord can change your responses in your life?



3. Reflect on this next verse from Paul's letter to the Romans:

   "Don't copy the behavior and customs of this world, but let God transform you into a new person by changing the way you think. Then you will learn to know God's will for you, which is good and pleasing and perfect" (Romans 12:2).



### A Three-Pronged Approach:

Part of healthier coping is caring for your mind, body, and spirit.

1.  What do you think you could do to better take care of your body?



2. What are some things you can do to take care of your spirit?

3. Lastly, from what you have learned in this study, what can you do to better care for your mind?

### Scripture's Role in Healthy Coping

Look up and reflect on the verses below:

Ephesians 5:29                                      3 John 1:2

When we address our minds, bodies, and spirits, we can better work on our coping mechanisms.

Reflect on the Scripture below before ending this day with your prayers and praises!

> "Therefore, since we are surrounded by such a huge crowd of witnesses to the life of faith, let us strip off every weight that slows us down, especially the sin that so easily trips us up. And let us run with endurance the race God has set before us. We do this by keeping our eyes on Jesus, the champion who initiates and perfects our faith. Because of the joy awaiting him, he endured the cross, disregarding its shame. Now he is seated in the place of honor beside God's throne" (Hebrews 12:1–2).

# Check-In and Homework Time

# Part Three: What Approach Are You Operating In?

When considering Outlaw, Scoundrel, and Partner Approach, your objective is to consistently operate in Partner Approach. However, as you and I navigate a complex world, there will be times when we find ourselves in Outlaw Approach and occasionally even in Scoundrel Approach, which is characterized by narcissistic behavior.

Outlaw Approach is activated when your relational circuits are turned off; this results in frustration, moodiness, a short temper, or even withdrawal.

1. When do you notice yourself operating in Outlaw Approach?

2. Look up Proverbs 14:29 NLT and reflect on how God's Word speaks to this very concept of Outlaw Approach.

It's normal to feel anger and other difficult emotions toward others and even yourself. However, it's your response to these feelings that determines whether you act foolishly. God understands that you will struggle and need to work on your behavior; this is no secret to Him.

Perhaps your first reaction is to say, "I couldn't possibly be a Scoundrel; I don't have any narcissistic behaviors!" Well, I have news for you: We can all operate in Scoundrel Approach from time to time. None of us is off limits from the Enemy's Scoundrels attacking us. Believe it or not, our relational circuits are very much active in Scoundrel Approach, but not for the right reasons. You can find yourself in this approach when you look for weaknesses in others, justify your poor behaviors by needing to be right, or act strategically in how you treat people for your own personal gain. This also occurs when you take advantage of others on purpose.

3. Look up and reflect on Philippians 2:3–4 NLT.

You and I can be the Outlaws or even Scoundrels when we are involved in an argument and are determined to be right. You may tend to adopt those approaches when you are avoiding responsibility and trying to blame others. In marriage, it's easy to be selfish because marriage tests generosity. This is why we often hear the saying that marriage is challenging and requires us to put our spouses before ourselves. The reason behind this is that the Enemy thrives on our selfishness. When you fall into being an Outlaw or a Scoundrel, you're exactly where he wants you!

Partner Approach is ideal—I wish we could continuously operate in this healthy mindset. In this approach, we are attuned to our relational circuits and bring pleasant energy to those around us. While it isn't realistic to think you can always be in Partner Approach,

it is something you should strive for. The more you build your joy centers, activate your relational circuits, and focus on growing closer to God, the more frequently you will find yourself in Partner Approach. I am sure that all of us would prefer to hear "Hey, Partner!" rather than "Hey, Outlaw!" or "Hey, Scoundrel!"

4. Can you think of a time you acted like a no-good Outlaw or, dare I ask, a nasty Scoundrel?

5. Look up and reflect on Proverbs 24:17.

## Check-In and Homework Time

## Part Four: My Personal Round-Up Story

Not too long ago, God revealed to me the immense need for tools to help us process everything going on in our lives. Now that we're in the final unit of this study, you *must* know I love a fun way to approach these things so that we can truly remember them. That moment when I felt God's push for memory tools was when the concept of the Round-Up was placed on my heart, and I am so thankful for it.

While writing this book, I encountered a particularly challenging time that caused me a great deal of stress and triggered difficult emotions. God made it clear that this was the perfect moment to apply a Round-Up. This included taking a moment to say, "WHOA," finding a safe place to work through my feelings alone, and crying so hard that I recognized the need for a STABLE to calm and gather myself.

After that, I was able to LASSO my trigger, which brought me to a place where I could take the time to do a HOWDY to connect more relationally with the Holy Spirit. Once I had done that, I started feeling considerably better and knew I needed a more joyful mindset to continue writing this book. So I decided to do a YEEHAW.

For my YEEHAW, I reflected on a recent shopping day with my oldest daughter Linden, during which we bought her prom dress. It was a special day filled with joy that we shared

with her friends and family. I cherished the moments of watching her try on dresses and the joy that illuminated all our faces each time she came out of the dressing room. When she finally said yes to the dress, I felt a tear roll down my cheek, overwhelmed by the beauty of experiencing that moment with her. We truly enjoyed each other that day!

Later on in that day I did a Tip My Hat and gave gratitude to the Lord for getting my mind in a functioning and clear state to be able to write my book. I also thanked Him because, as I wrote for hours, He worked on the heart of the loved one that upset me so much. The person even apologized. I was in awe that the Round-Up not only got me functioning but also left room for God to fix the issue I was having rather than allowing me to try to control it. I had lots to be grateful for!

The Round-Up process helped me reach a functional and clear space to keep writing my book. Although I still had unresolved issues, I also felt a perfect peace knowing I had given it all to God.

My hope is that when life throws stress or pain your way, you can pause and say, "WHOA" and begin the Round-Up process. It's all about retraining yourself for better coping mechanisms, and I can say that to you with a clear heart and mind because of how I have grown from practicing new methods.

At times, you may need to perform a complete Round-Up, or you might only need to perform one or two steps. Pay attention to your body and do what feels necessary. Take a moment to review Round-Up techniques now!

## WHOA

**W** — WAIT BEFORE RESPONDING. CONSIDER WHETHER YOU'RE BEING HOWDY OR ROWDY. ARE YOU TRIGGERED?

**H** — HOLY SPIRIT. LISTEN FOR HIS SOFT VOICE. PRAY.

**O** — OBSERVE HOW YOU ARE FEELING.

**A** — ACTION MAY BE NEEDED. CHOOSE IF YOU NEED TO GET STABLE (THINK BACK TO THE IMAGE FROM THE TRAIL TO HEALING) OR IF YOU ARE IN A HEALTHY PLACE TO RESPOND.

## THE LASSO

ROOT

BULLIED

CHILDHOOD WOUND

REJECTION

FEEL NEGLECTED

MISUNDERSTOOD

TOXIC SHAME

FEEL ABANDONED

BURIED TRAUMA

PAST ABUSE

## YEEHAW

**Y** — YOU CAN FIND JOY. TELL YOURSELF THAT!

**E** — ENGAGE WITH THE HOLY SPIRIT. BE STILL AND LISTEN.

**E** — ENCOURAGE YOURSELF TO RECALL A JOYFUL MOMENT OF GRATITUDE FROM YOUR MEMORY.

**H** — HOLD ONTO THAT MOMENT AS LONG AS YOU CAN, UP TO FIVE MINUTES.

**A** — ASSESS HOW YOU FEEL IN YOUR MIND AND BODY.

**W** — WELCOME THE FEELING OF JOY AND GIVE THE LORD GRATITUDE.

## STABLE

**S** — SAFE PLACE, AS IN GO TO A SAFE PLACE AND LET YOURSELF FEEL THE EMOTIONS.

**T** — TAKE A MOMENT TO RESET YOUR BRAIN THROUGH BREATHING, GRATITUDE, OR WORSHIP MUSIC.

**A** — ASK FOR THE HOLY SPIRIT'S HELP IN UNDERSTANDING HOW YOU ARE FEELING.

**B** — BRING TRUTH TO YOUR EMOTIONS; LOOK UP SCRIPTURE ON HOW YOU ARE FEELING

**L** — LIST WAYS YOU CAN BETTER MOVE FORWARD: DO A LASSO, HOWDY, AND YEEHAW OR SEEK HELP.

**E** — END IN A CALMER STATE.

## HOWDY

**H** — HOLY SPIRIT TIME! TAKE TIME TO BE STILL, PRAY, AND LISTEN.

"Howdy, Holy Spirit..."

**O** — OBSERVE AND WRITE WHAT YOU ARE HEARING AND FEELING.

**W** — WHAT DOES GOD'S WORD SAY? READ AND REFLECT ON SCRIPTURE.

**D** — DISCOVER (ASK, SEEK, AND WRITE) WHAT THE HOLY SPIRIT HAS FOR YOU TO DO TODAY!

**Y** — YES! YOU CAN DO WHAT HE LEADS YOU TO ACCOMPLISH!

*Don't forget to give prayer requests and praises!*

### TIP YOUR HAT to Jesus and say, "Much obliged!"

BE STILL WITH THE HOLY SPIRIT AND ASK HIM TO GIVE YOU A MEMORY THAT YOU ARE THANKFUL FOR.

WRITE THAT MEMORY OUT AND THANK GOD FOR IT!

TAKE TIME TO WRITE WHAT YOU THINK GOD IS SHOWING YOU THROUGH THAT EXPERIENCE.

CAN YOU CONNECT THIS MOMENT TO A SPECIFIC SCRIPTURE? IF SO, MAKE A NOTE OF THAT ALSO.

SIT STILL AND ALLOW YOURSELF TO FEEL GRATEFUL FOR THAT EXPERIENCE!

TIP YOUR HAT TO JESUS ONCE A DAY!

The word WHOA and the four steps associated with it are a helpful reminder to take a pause. I encourage you to start practicing this technique. If you struggle with this, please know that you're not alone.

1. Can you pause before reacting or during reactions to better manage yourself and your situation?

The STABLE encourages us to reach a stable, calm place. Look up and reflect on John 14:27. True peace and calm come from the Lord.

2. Is it hard to find calm in the midst of stress or a trigger?

The LASSO concept helps bring awareness to a trigger's root. Once you identify that root, you can better heal. For me, an example of lassoing a root goes back to a mean girl in middle school who was considered Miss Popular. She cycled through friends often. I remember the day she noticed me, and we became close. I felt so important until she publicly ditched me, making me look foolish in front of a group of people. Throughout my healing process, I realized that this incident had a lasting impact on my life. It affected my thoughts about my worthiness within true friendships. That experience made me even more shy throughout school and caused me to distrust people. Ultimately, I was able to uncover the root of my struggle, and God is working on me to be more trusting of friendships.

When I reflect on universal life experiences, it's clear that many carry wounds that need healing. It's important to recognize that when you feel triggered, there's often a deeper reason behind that reaction. Start paying attention to these triggers and use a LASSO technique to uncover the root of your feelings. Once you have lassoed the trigger, take a moment to connect with the Holy Spirit through a HOWDY. This helps you establish a deeper connection with God. Then follow up with a YEEHAW to uplift your spirits and return to a more joyful state! Finally, finish up by doing a Tip My Hat; give gratitude to Jesus and strengthen your connection with Him even more.

I pray that these methods can be helpful in your life.

# Checking In on FBEAP – Foundational Principle: Push/Pull

Here is a personal Push/Pull story of my own. For about a year, my daughter Sutton had wanted me to take her ice skating. I skated competitively as a child, so she wanted to experience skating with me. She had already gone with some friends and discovered that she was quite the natural, so she wanted to show me her skills.

However, after being sick for years, I had lost confidence in my skating abilities. Every time Sutton asked me to go, I would come up with excuses to avoid it. God was working on me to have an "I can" mentality, so it became clear to me, especially when our church was hosting a youth skating event, that I should join Sutton.

When we arrived, my children announced to everyone that I knew how to skate, which added pressure. As I laced up my skates, I felt a mix of excitement and nerves. When it was time to step onto the ice, I hesitated, feeling a pit in my stomach, and pulled back, walking away from the entrance. Then I ran into my precious niece Ella and confided, "I'm so scared! What if I can't still skate?" She looked at me and said, "Aunt Melissa, you will be better than me because I don't know how." With that, she continued toward the entrance of the ice arena.

At that moment, I thought to myself, *If Ella can get on that ice, so can I*. I decided to *push* through my fear of making a fool of myself and stepped onto the ice. At first, I definitely felt rusty and thought, *Oh boy, this could be interesting*. But I kept *pushing* forward, and before I knew it, my muscle memory kicked in, and I realized I could still skate. I got to skate alongside Sutton, who was whizzing around the rink just like her mother.

Before long, I was doing spins and jumps! The neatest part was teaching Sutton and Ella how to skate. Can you imagine how much joy I would have missed if I hadn't *pushed* through my fears and participated? I'm so glad I did!

In my story, *pulling* back was an essential movement for me as I needed more encouragement from Ella to skate. You see, we will *pull* back in life, but it's what we do afterward that matters. We must *push* forward.

1. Do you feel anything in your life that you keep *pulling* back from, and as a result you're not experiencing all God has for you?

2. Look up and reflect on Isaiah 41:10–13.

God will help us *push* forward! Indeed, He may even hold your right hand—are you brave enough to ask Him to?

Have you said howdy to the Holy Spirit today and checked in with Him? Or, like me on some of my off days, did you find yourself scrolling through your phone for thirty minutes?

Have you expressed a joyful YEEHAW? This simple act will help you and me to build our joy centers and allow us to cope more effectively with life's challenges. Making this a daily habit is vital for navigating life's journey!

Finally, did you have a Tip My Hat moment where you shared deep gratitude with the Lord?

Healing and living a life illuminated by the Holy Spirit entails checking in with Him daily, diving into His Word, and cherishing quality time together. When you nurture your spirit with the Holy Spirit, you'll always find your way!

As Charles Stanley once said, "If we walk in the Spirit daily, surrendered to His power, we have the right to expect anything we need to hear from God. The Holy Spirit living within us and speaking to us ought to be the natural, normal lifestyle of believers."

We can't establish a better habit than checking in and saying howdy to the Holy Spirit, celebrating with a YEEHAW every day, and following with a Tip My Hat to express gratitude. I've included a check-in page for you to use as you start your HOWDY and YEEHAW journey!

**H** HOLY SPIRIT TIME! TAKE TIME TO BE STILL, PRAY, AND LISTEN.

**O** OBSERVE AND WRITE WHAT YOU ARE HEARING AND FEELING.

*"Howdy, Holy Spirit..."*

**W** WHAT DOES GOD'S WORD SAY? READ AND REFLECT ON SCRIPTURE.

**D** DISCOVER (ASK, SEEK, AND WRITE) WHAT THE HOLY SPIRIT HAS FOR YOU TO DO TODAY!

**Y** YES! YOU CAN DO WHAT HE LEADS YOU TO ACCOMPLISH!

*Don't forget to give prayer requests and praises!*

---

**H** HOLY SPIRIT TIME! TAKE TIME TO BE STILL, PRAY, AND LISTEN.

**O-**

**W-**

**D-**

**Y** YES! I CAN DO WHAT HE LEADS ME TO ACCOMPLISH!

*Don't forget prayer requests and to give praises!*

**Y** YOU CAN FIND JOY.
TELL YOURSELF THAT!

**E** ENGAGE WITH THE HOLY SPIRIT.
BE STILL AND LISTEN.

**E** ENCOURAGE YOURSELF TO RECALL A JOYFUL
MOMENT OF GRATITUDE FROM YOUR MEMORY.

**H** HOLD ONTO THAT MOMENT AS LONG
AS YOU CAN, UP TO FIVE MINUTES.

**A** ASSESS HOW YOU FEEL IN YOUR
MIND AND BODY.

**W** WELCOME THE FEELING OF JOY
AND GIVE THE LORD GRATITUDE.

**Y** YOU CAN FIND JOY!

**E-**

**E-**

**H** HOLD ONTO THE MOMENT.

**A-**

**W-**

★ ★ ★

TIP YOUR HAT
to
Jesus
and say,
"Much obliged!"

BE STILL WITH THE HOLY SPIRIT AND ASK HIM TO GIVE YOU A MEMORY THAT YOU ARE THANKFUL FOR.

WRITE THAT MEMORY OUT AND THANK GOD FOR IT!

TAKE TIME TO WRITE WHAT YOU THINK GOD IS SHOWING YOU THROUGH THAT EXPERIENCE.

CAN YOU CONNECT THIS MOMENT TO A SPECIFIC SCRIPTURE? IF SO, MAKE A NOTE OF THAT ALSO.

SIT STILL AND ALLOW YOURSELF TO FEEL GRATEFUL FOR THAT EXPERIENCE!

TIP YOUR HAT TO JESUS ONCE A DAY!

TRY TO SHARE WRITTEN GRATITUDES WITH LOVED ONES REGULARLY!

★ ★ ★

# Prayers and Praises

# It's time for
# Conclusion

# It's time for an
# Introduction
# of the final
## FBEAP Philosophy

## It's Time to Introduce the Final FBEAP – Foundational Principle:

# Attention and At Ease

The last philosophy of FBEAP that I want to discuss is Attention and At Ease. I believe it's fitting to introduce this concept at the end because, ultimately, even God rested after creation. Why does God command us to rest on the Sabbath? I believe it's to prevent us from becoming so busy that we burn out and to encourage us to spend quality time resting with Him. In a world that promotes the idea of "more, more, more," it's easy to feel overwhelmed and experience burnout.

## An Example of Attention and At Ease

Providing for our families in 2025 is more challenging than it was in 2019. Families must work harder to pay bills and secure a stable future. The drive to provide shows your attention to a need, an essential survival skill. However, are you also taking the time to be at ease? Being at ease means taking time to rest and recharge. We can't heal from an empty cup. I understand that it can be challenging to prioritize rest, but it's important to remember that when we rush through without taking the time to recharge, we can unintentionally develop unhealthy ways to cope; this can also create burnout. Taking care of yourself is essential.

Please refer to the next page for an illustration of the concept of Attention and At Ease.

**SECURITY**

BEING ATTENTIVE IS AN IMPORTANT SURVIVAL SKILL. HORSE HERDS RELY ON IT TO KEEP THEM SAFE. WE PAY ATTENTION FOR THE SAME REASONS.

**REST**

BEING AT EASE IS IMPORTANT BECAUSE WE NEED TO REST AND HAVE TIME TO BE CALM.

In horse herds, you can often observe when they are alert and attentive. Sometimes, there may be one horse that is consistently vigilant, taking the time to ensure the herd's safety. You will also see the horses grazing and resting, which is crucial for their well-being. Just as Jesus was always attentive to God's guidance, He also took time to rest. Being at ease means striving for a healthy, balanced life.[85]

---

85    Davis, *Foundations*, 25.

★ ★ ★

# Check-In and Homework Time

1. How well do you stay attentive to what's going on around you? Are you on top of things, too attentive, or in a place of checking out?

2. Reflect on the passage below. What can you take away from the Word here?

> "Guard your heart above all else,
>> for it determines the course of your life.
> Avoid all perverse talk;
>> stay away from corrupt speech.
> Look straight ahead,
>> and fix your eyes on what lies before you.
> Mark out a straight path for your feet;
>> stay on the safe path.
> Don't get sidetracked;
>> keep your feet from following evil."
> (Proverbs 4:23–27)

3. Being attentive and not getting sidetracked are essential to staying on the path. But we must also remember to rest and be still with the Lord! Read this psalm and then try to recall a time when God gave you the peace to rest.

   "In peace I will lie down and sleep, for you alone, Lord, make me dwell in safety" (Psalm 4:8).

4. True peace and rest come from the Lord. Is it hard for you to take time to rest?

★ ★ ★

"There remains, then, a Sabbath-rest for the people of God; for anyone who enters God's rest also rests from their works, just as God did from his. Let us, therefore, make every effort to enter that rest, so that no one will perish by following their example of disobedience" (Hebrews 4:9–11 NIV).

Whoa! God clearly indicates that we are in disobedience when we neglect to rest. That can be quite convicting. However, from my own experience on my healing journey, I can say that life becomes so much more rewarding when I take time to rest my body and spend time with God. We must care for ourselves!

The terms *Attention* and *At Ease* come into a new light when you can view them through the lens of Scripture. There is a time for your attention, most definitely. As I wrote earlier, the drive to provide for your family is good. At the same time, the need to rest and be at ease is necessary for growth and healing.

As our journey comes to a close, I pray you have learned the importance of taking care of your mind, body, and spirit so that you can fulfill all that God has called you to be. Don't let the guilt and busyness of this world prevent you from resting with God and continuing on your healing journey!

We've shared an amazing journey together. As I write these words, I am filled with emotion as I reflect on how faithful God has been in granting me the wisdom and inspiration to write this book. I hope that it will touch countless lives here at Our Healing Farm and all throughout the world! I want this book to become a cherished memory for you as you apply its teachings in your life.

I encourage you to spread the message that healing is possible and to share the insights you've gained with your loved ones. Healing from past trauma and learning to live in a way that is truly in sync with the Holy Spirit will allow you and me to fulfill the Great Commission. Just as Jesus said to His disciples, "Therefore go and make disciples of all nations, baptizing them in the name of the Father and of the Son and of the Holy Spirit, and teaching them to obey everything I have commanded you. And surely I am with you always, to the very end of the age" (Matthew 28:19–20 NIV). When we obey His commands, we will be healed and create communities that mimic the herds He intended.

I truly hope you have begun a healing process, and I look forward to hearing about the wonderful things God will do in your life. May you develop a deep desire to learn more about healing. I cannot thank you enough for allowing me to be a part of your journey.

With love, *Melissa Prusinski*

# My Testimony

## A Chance to Give Glory to God's Faithfulness

Friend, the end of our trail is just the beginning of another. Since you have done the work that leads to healing, I want to spur you on! My hope and prayer is that you will continue deepening your relationship with our triune God. The following pages are my testimony of God's faithfulness in my life. After reading this very honest account, perhaps you can write your own. "And let us consider how we may spur one another on toward love and good deeds" (Hebrews 10:24 NIV)!

How does a girl raised in a subdivision of a Midwest town end up writing a Western-themed book on trauma healing that incorporates horses? If someone had told little me that this would happen, I wouldn't have believed it. Growing up wasn't the picture-perfect suburban dream that some people envision in movies. While there were streets lined with houses and kids riding bikes and playing, my childhood was filled with a lot of pain behind closed doors.

My parents rarely got along, and both carried their own unhealed childhood traumas, which they didn't know how to manage. This challenging environment contributed to my becoming a chronic people-pleaser, a habit I am currently working to heal. I struggled with childhood anxiety and developed poor coping mechanisms from a young age. My mother, a believer, tried several times to take us to church, but my father, who had experienced significant religious abuse in his past, wanted nothing to do with God. Hearing my dad's stories about how Christians treated him, along with witnessing it myself, made it clear to me at a young age that I wanted nothing to do with that.

During my high school years, I became caught up in the excitement of relationships at a young age. As I reached my later teens, I found myself in a toxic relationship that was both mentally and sexually harmful. It wasn't until I engaged in trauma healing later in life that I truly understood the extent of the many emotional wounds it had left me with.

Having dealt with ADD symptoms throughout childhood, when I went to college, I learned real fast that it wasn't for me. I couldn't retain information or pay attention, so I decided to put my more artistic brain to use and get my cosmetologist license. In beauty school, a friend I met there introduced me to my husband, Blake.

Blake, a small-town country boy, grew up in a strict, cult-like religion, but he did understand the fundamental concept of salvation. I'll never forget the day we were at Olive Garden on a date, and he looked at me and said that we were both going to hell because being a good person isn't enough; you must be saved. To be honest, he could have approached the topic with more sensitivity, but it's important to remember that he was raised in a very legalistic environment. As a result, he believed he was too imperfect to achieve salvation.

When we got engaged, the same friends who introduced us invited us to church. We needed a place to get married, so we thought, *Why not?* In that pew, I heard the true message of Jesus, one that embraces you as you are, and I gave my life to Him, inviting Him into my heart. Blake took longer to come to this decision because of the toxic beliefs ingrained in the cult.

For years, we struggled financially while we were married. We understood what it was like to live with uncertainty, not knowing how our bills would be paid. Living in a rural area meant high-income trade jobs were few and far between. Eventually, feeling overwhelmed by our struggles, Blake took some wise advice to heart: "You will never be perfect, and God wants you just as you are." He decided to give his life to the Lord. While we continued to face challenges, the burden felt lighter because we had God to help us carry it. A couple of years later, Blake began an apprenticeship to become a journeyman lineman, and we were financially blessed.

Life was going well; we had our first daughter, Linden, and were enjoying raising her. While we attended church, I would say our faith was growing slowly, a tendency that often occurs when things are going smoothly.

When we decided to have a second child, we faced one of our biggest trials as a couple: experiencing multiple miscarriages in a row. It was an incredibly devastating period, and amid the pain, I lost friendships that once meant the world to me. This was truly one of the most painful times of our lives, which taught me that in times of trial, the only source of comfort I could rely on was God. No human could provide the solace I needed; people can fail us, but God never will.

This journey involved seeking answers for our losses, which led to various treatments and supplementary medications. Once we identified the issues, we were ultimately blessed with the arrival of our second daughter, Sutton.

While we were enduring that kind of pain, God sent a solid pastor and his wife into our lives, which greatly strengthened our relationship with the Lord. One Sunday, during an altar call, the pastor asked, "Will you do all God asks of you in your life?" Both Blake and I went up, fully submitting to Him. I'll never forget that the song "I Have Decided to Follow

Jesus" played that day. Experiencing loss teaches you what is truly important. Soon after that altar call, God called Blake and me to move to California for work to help pay off our house in Michigan and get us living debt-free.

When we traveled to California for the hiring meeting, I remember leaving with the thought, *I never want to live here.* The pace of life was too fast and outside of my comfort zone. Blake felt the same way. However, we couldn't ignore the strong sense that we were meant to go. So we packed up our two young daughters and Great Dane, rented our house, and moved to a Residence Inn in California while Blake completed his training. We were truly on a journey led by the Holy Spirit.

Did you notice a potential problem with what we had packed? Imagine trying to rent a house with a Great Dane—no one wanted to rent to us! Our time at the hotel was ending, and we needed a place to live. Then I remembered something my dad had said before we left: "Maybe you should consider living in an RV since it's temporary." I laughed and dismissed the idea, thinking it was crazy, especially since it wasn't the trendy thing to do back then.

But one night, I was awakened, dreaming about RVs. I told Blake, "I hate to suggest this, but maybe we're meant to live in an RV?" We both decided to look for a safe RV park where we could stay. I prayed, asking God to show us exactly where He wanted us. I heard a still voice say it would feel like home—calm, country-like, and a sense of community. I thought, *How is that possible in this part of California?*

When we drove to the first RV park recommended by a guy from Blake's work, we found it was completely booked, and we were put on a waitlist. It didn't feel like home; it felt like a concrete jungle. The friend told Blake there was also a place next door, but it wasn't as nice, and he wasn't sure we would like it.

When we arrived at the second RV park, the roads were dirt, lined with eucalyptus trees throughout the park. It felt like the countryside and was calm and peaceful. I smiled and looked up to the Lord, knowing this was home.

That little RV park became our home for nearly two years, where we formed a community of friends on similar journeys. Just a week after moving in, I walked alongside a new friend who was coping with a devastating miscarriage. It was clear that God had placed us right where we needed to be.

He led us to a wonderful church that embodied the spirit of being relational and welcoming to our family. Our time in California led to significant personal growth. However, it wasn't easy living in a small space, being away from family, and having Blake work so much.

To combat loneliness, my daughters and I enjoyed watching the TV show *Heartland*. My girls became obsessed with horses and told Blake and me they wanted a horse when we moved back to Michigan. Although Blake had grown up having horses and showing cattle for 4-H, he referred to horses as "hay burners" and said, "Never will happen!"

I remember watching *Heartland* one day and feeling robbed in my life. The show felt so healing, yet I had never been around a horse. My heart ached for something I could never have.

Once the house was paid off, we sold the RV and went home.

The girls didn't take long to convince us to get a horse since we owned land. Blake lost that battle three to one!

I'll never forget the day we responded to a Craigslist ad for a small paint horse named Behr. He desperately needed a home because his family was going through a divorce, and the owner had run out of hay. Behr was hungry, and his body showed it. His eyes were so kind, and he tolerated the kids leading him around. We decided we couldn't leave him there, so he came home with us.

Not long after Behr arrived home, we realized he had experienced some trauma in his past. He would run away from us, hated men, and didn't want the kids to ride him. However, he did seem to like one person: me. At that point, I was completely drawn to that little paint horse and learned to ride him. He became mine, and we reached an understanding that I would never hurt him.

We decided to get him a miniature horse as a companion and for the girls to ride. So we went to look at a miniature horse that a local family was selling. When we entered the barn, we saw a morbidly obese horse that was spending its life standing, eating, and staying in a dark barn all day. Understandably, we couldn't leave him there, so Boris came home with us.

Horses quickly became my new passion; I was completely hooked. We loved spending time with them and soon realized we needed more property than we currently had. We were outgrowing our land. Unfortunately, no land was available around our home, so we decided that if God presented us with property, we would move. Blake started a sawmill as a hobby, with the intention of building us a house using the lumber he cut. We began dreaming of creating a rustic farm.

One day, Blake was driving his work truck when he spotted a small "For Sale By Owner" sign down a quiet dirt road that advertised forty acres for sale. That night, he took me to

see it. I had always dreamed of living on a quiet road lined with trees, and I was in awe when he turned down that dirt lane, where beautiful hard maples formed a canopy above, displaying stunning colors. I looked at him and said, "Sold." After seeing the property, I enthusiastically repeated, "Sold again." We felt truly blessed by God to have found it. We decided that one day we would build our dream home on this land. Our neighbor heard that we had purchased the property and offered to buy our current house, allowing us to continue living there until we built our new place. We accepted the offer and sold our home.

When life seemed poised for a significant change, Blake traveled to California for seasonal work, with plans to return home to build a barn with living quarters. While we were out visiting him, we faced one of our biggest challenges: I fell seriously ill. My health deteriorated rapidly, starting with poor vision and quickly escalating to being bedridden within three months.

It turned out that my decision to get breast implants stirred up an underlying issue in my body—Lyme disease. When I was twelve, I had a tick removed from my ear, but we never realized that I had contracted Lyme disease. I had experienced bouts of chronic illness since then, but had no idea I had Lyme. One of the implants developed a small air leak, which poisoned my body at an alarming rate. I became extremely toxic and was unable to function.

After a year of not knowing I had Lyme disease, plus dealing with breast implant illness, I opted to have my implants removed, hoping to find answers. Unfortunately, this decision left me even sicker as my body was already so weak from the Lyme that it couldn't handle the surgery. When I finally received the Lyme diagnosis six months post-surgery, I was suffering from seizures, brain fog, significant weight loss, debilitating fatigue, memory loss, severe body aches, and many more symptoms. This was undoubtedly the most challenging experience I've ever had to endure.

To treat my late-stage neurological Lyme disease, I spent fourteen months on IV antibiotics and received home health care, along with various holistic treatments to help me regain my health.

During the seven years of my illness, we took in five more horses: a retired draft team that Blake desired (despite his initial reluctance to keep "hay burners"), another mini horse, a large pony, and a quarter horse. Our daughters became involved in horse shows, and our connection to the horse world only grew stronger. Throughout my illness, Blake continued to build and expand, creating a beautiful, rustic horse farm.

Although I was better functioning after four years of being sick, I had not yet healed my mind. One night, I was reminded of a *Focus on the Family* episode featuring Kim Meeker,

which discussed the healing abilities of horses when used by God. When I looked her up, I found that her education class was at capacity, so I kept searching, and that's when I discovered Unbridled™ with Elaine Davis. I felt a strong encouragement from the Holy Spirit to attend as it was a certification program focused on trauma healing using the Holy Spirit and horses.

So we traveled to Minnesota, and that trip changed my life forever. During the experience, I realized I was riddled with trauma, which led me to a three-year journey of healing my mind and spirit. This involved participating in support groups with Door of Hope and receiving some counseling. I was introduced to The Life Model, which profoundly transformed my life.

In 2024, I began ministry work using FBEAP, and it's become one of the most satisfying experiences of my life. I feel beyond blessed by the Lord.

One day, after a long day of ministry work, I was walking through my house when God stopped me in my tracks. He reminded me of the memory in California where I felt robbed watching *Heartland*. He made it clear that I now have my own unique version of the *Heartland* farm right here at Our Healing Farm and that nothing is impossible—and it's never too late to start something new! God is so good!

As I prepared for our ministry, the Lord placed it on my heart to write a book to accompany our work—something fun, something easy to grasp and remember. My brain and many others need that. So that is how this book came to be. He also inspired me to produce it on a wide scale as it can still help people who do not have access to FBEAP. While the horses provide a remarkable healing aspect, this book is also healing in its own right.

Can you imagine all we would have missed if we hadn't answered the call to California? We left our comfortable lives to live Holy Spirit-led. There were certainly extreme challenges and mistakes along the way, but God used those trials to grow us. I wouldn't change a thing.

My dream for this book, and the vulnerability that comes with sharing my testimony, is that many will awaken to healing from trauma with the Holy Spirit guiding them, allowing them to live the joyful lives we are all called to live!

*Melissa*

# Recommended Resources and Organizations

Coursey, Chris. *The Joy Switch: How Your Brain's Secret Circuit Affects Your Relationships—And How You Can Activate It.* Moody Publishers, 2021.

Friesen, James, James E. Wilder, Anne Bierling, Rick Koepke, and Maribeth Poole. *Living From the Heart Jesus Gave You.* Shepherd's House, 2016.

Hendricks, Michel, and Jim Wilder. *The Other Half of Church.* Moody Publishers, 2020.

Lehman, Karl. *Outsmarting Yourself: Catching Your Past Invading the Present and What to Do about It.* 2nd ed. Immanuel Publishing, 2014.

Warner, Marcus, and Chris Coursey. *The 4 Habits of Joy-Filled People.* Northfield Publishing, 2023.

Wilder, E. James, Anna Kang, John Loppnow, and Sungshim Loppnow. *Joyful Journey: Listening to Immanuel.* Presence and Practice, 2020.

Wilder, E. James, Edward Khouri, Chris Coursey, and Sheila Sutton. *Joy Starts Here.* Life Model Works™, 2021.

lifemodelworks.org — Life Model connects neuroscience with biblical teachings to develop straightforward, practical resources for churches to foster genuine community and facilitate life transformation.

doorofhopeministries.org — Door of Hope provides support groups, prayer recovery, and professional counseling to assist in the healing process. They utilize the Life Model Works™ and the Immanuel Approach in their ministry. This organization has provided resources supporting my family and me today.

aliveandwell.org — Alive and Well offers journey groups.

https://debrafileta.com/counseling/ — The Debra Fileta Counselors Network offers online professional Christian counseling.

https://www.unbridledfaith.org/ — Unbridled™ Faith-Based Equine Assisted Philosophy: This is an opportunity for anyone interested in becoming certified in FBEAP.